Pure Poetry

Death Poetry

"Death, Be Not Proud"

Stephanie Buckwalter

 Enslow Publishers, Inc.
40 Industrial Road
Box 398
Berkeley Heights, NJ 07922
USA
http://www.enslow.com

Library of Congress Cataloging-in-Publication Data

Buckwalter, Stephanie.

 Death poetry : "Death, be not proud" / Stephanie Buckwalter.
   pages cm. — (Pure Poetry)
 Includes bibliographical references and index.
 Summary: "Explores death poetry, including famous American and European poets and
   their poems, as well as literary criticism, poetic technique, explication, and prompts for
   further study"—Provided by publisher.
 ISBN 978-0-7660-4257-5
 1. Poetry—History and criticism—Juvenile literature. 2. Death in literature. 3. Elegiac
   poetry—History and criticism—Juvenile literature. I. Title.
 PN1083.D43B83 2013
 809.1'93548—dc23
                        2013008360

Future editions:
Paperback ISBN: 978-1-4644-0457-3
EPUB ISBN: 978-1-4645-1248-3
Single-User PDF ISBN: 978-1-4646-1248-0
Multi-User PDF ISBN: 978-0-7660-5880-4

Printed in the United States of America

112013 Lake Book Manufacturing, Inc., Melrose Park, IL

10 9 8 7 6 5 4 3 2 1

To Our Readers: We have done our best to make sure all Internet addresses in this book
were active and appropriate when we went to press. However, the author and the publisher
have no control over and assume no liability for the material available on those Internet sites
or on other Web sites they may link to. Any comments or suggestions can be sent by e-mail
to comments@enslow.com or to the address on the back cover.

♻ Enslow Publishers, Inc., is committed to printing our books on recycled paper. The paper
in every book contains 10% to 30% post-consumer waste (PCW). The cover board on the
outside of each book contains 100% PCW. Our goal is to do our part to help young people
and the environment too!

Photo and Illustration Credits: © Clipart.com, pp. 13, 29; Engraving by George E.
Perine & Co., reproduced from the *Dictionary of American Portraits*, published by Dover
Publications, Inc., in 1967, p. 92; Library of Congress, pp. 54, 75; © Photos.com, p. 69;
Public Domain, pp. 38, 106.

Cover Illustration: Shutterstock.com.

Contents

Introduction

Is death the end—or a new beginning? Should it be feared—or embraced? Or is it simply a ceasing to exist? Poets like to contemplate the deep mysteries of life, especially things like death that cannot be fully known. Good poets will draw you into their thoughts and take you on a journey. These journeys are often filled with surprises and shaded with self-realization. Each of the poems presented in this book gives a different view of death. They span three centuries and two countries and capture both the ideas of the time and the concerns of the poets.

There are two schools of thought in analyzing poetry. Some critics believe a poem should stand on its own with no need for knowledge of outside events or the poet's life. Other critics believe the full meaning of the poem can only be grasped by understanding the circumstances under which it was written. Several of the poems in this book can be understood independent of context, such as "We Are Seven" and "Because I Could Not Stop for Death." But for others, such as "The Charge of the Light Brigade" and "Vigil Strange I Kept on the Field One Night," it is almost necessary to know about the time and place to gain a full appreciation of its meaning. This book provides the context of all the poems as well as one or more possible interpretations.

Throughout history, there have been distinct phases of literary thought and technique. They are called by various names, such as eras, ages, or periods. Those labels can be used interchangeably. Each new era often grows out of, or is a reaction to, the previous era. For example, the Age of Enlightenment was all about logic and reason. It developed during a time of great scientific advancement in business—the Industrial Age. During the Industrial Age, people moved into the cities to work in the factories. Conditions were horrid both in the factories and in home life (think of Charles Dickens's works). What followed next was the Romantic Age, where emotions reigned supreme. The Romantic Era was about getting back in touch with nature and emotions in a world that often seemed cold and heartless.

The poems in this book are laid out in chronological order. The most challenging poem, published in 1633, is first. It requires an in-depth look at meter, which will help in analyzing the other poems. It also introduces nine different literary devices. The rest of the poems use fewer devices, making them easier to analyze. The questions at the end of each chapter will give you additional insights and provide an opportunity to work with the poem on your own.

In poetry, literary devices serve various purposes. Some literary devices, such as allusion and metaphor, are used as shorthand for meaning. For example, the poet may refer to something outside the poem, such as a war, to form an association without going into detail. He expects the reader to understand the reference and apply it to what the poem is saying. Other literary devices, such as alliteration, rhyme, and rhythm, create patterns of sound that can enhance the meaning of the words. Each of these devices will be explained as they occur. If the first poem, "Death, Be Not Proud," seems difficult to grasp, feel free to jump ahead and come back to it last. The other poems are less dense and use fewer literary devices. Once you've had practice analyzing some of the easier poems, the first one will not present such a challenge.

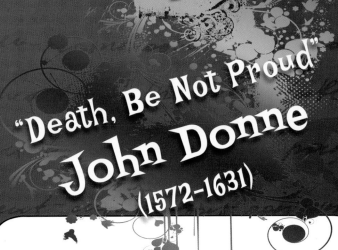

1

"Death, Be Not Proud" John Donne (1572-1631)

The title of the poem "Death, Be Not Proud" sounds strong and noble. But if it had a subtitle, it would be something like "An Insult to Death" or "The Great Verbal Smackdown." The poet relies on wit and sarcasm to cut death down to size. Even though people tend to revere history and historical figures, the truth is that human nature doesn't change from one age to the next. People of every age experience fear of death, show acts of courage, and express their wit. You will find shades of all of these in this poem.

A Reluctant Minister

John Donne's poetry reflects his struggle with his religion. Donne was born in London in 1572, into a Catholic family at a time when the Church of

The Metaphysical Poets

Donne is grouped in the Metaphysical poets, along with Andrew Marvell and George Herbert. Metaphysics is a branch of philosophy that predates the modern scientific era. Metaphysicists tried to explain life by observing the natural order of things around them. The Metaphysical poets were not called that while they lived but were later categorized based on their use of physical images and symbols to represent complex metaphysical concepts about God, creation, and the afterlife. Because Donne was a minister, he used many biblical references and based them on the idea of going to heaven once a person dies. The Metaphysical poets are specifically noted for their wit. They could talk about serious subjects while infusing them with humor. This poem is a great example. Think of *Monty Python and the Holy Grail*, where the French soldiers are taunting the English. This poem could easily be read in that vein.

England was persecuting Catholics for their beliefs. He was educated at Oxford and Cambridge but could not receive degrees due to his Catholic convictions. He then studied law. Upon leaving school, he went to work in London. He began writing poetry and published his first book of poems, *Satires*, during that time. When his career took a dive due to a secret marriage, and he was thrust into poverty for a while, he supported his family by writing for others.

Over time, his religious views changed. He publicly renounced his Catholic faith. He wrote a couple of pieces about how Catholics could pledge allegiance to King James I as head of the Anglican Church and still keep their conscience clear.

This, of course, caught the king's attention and gained his favor. In time, King James encouraged Donne to become an Anglican minister. The king "persuaded" him by threatening to remove his personal favor, which would have brought on a return to the poverty of his earlier years. Donne accepted. He became well known for his sermons filled with elaborate metaphors and religious symbolism. His deep thoughts, quick wit, and flair for drama made him one of the favorite preachers of the era.

Although he is now remembered for his poetry, he thought he would be remembered for his sermons. According to the editors of his ten-volume collection of sermons, he wrestled with the same things in both: the "sacred and secular: the relationship between matter and spirit, the fate of the soul, the tension between self-assertion and submission, paradox, and the negotiation of identity from contraries."[1]

In other words, he wanted to delve into the meaning of life and what happens after life.

Death, Be Not Proud
(Holy Sonnet X)

Death, be not proud, though some have called thee
Mighty and dreadful, for thou art not so;
For those whom thou think'st thou dost overthrow,
Die not, poor Death, nor yet canst thou kill me.
From rest and sleep, which but thy pictures be,
Much pleasure; then from thee much more must flow,
And soonest our best men with thee do go,
Rest of their bones, and soul's delivery.
Thou art slave to fate, chance, kings, and desperate men,
And dost with poison, war, and sickness dwell;
And poppy or charms can make us sleep as well
And better than thy stroke; why swell'st thou then?
One short sleep past, we wake eternally,
And death shall be no more; Death, thou shalt die.

Faith or Fear?

"Death, Be Not Proud" is number ten of the nineteen "Holy Sonnets" that Donne wrote, called holy because they dealt with religious themes. His conflicted religious beliefs often led him to wrestle with what he believed. This poem appears to be a reproach to death. It is unclear whether it is based on faith or on fear. If based on faith, it is a mere rebuke, putting death in its place. If it is based on fear, it is more like "whistling past the graveyard in the dark," where he is trying to talk himself into believing what he is saying. Donne was no stranger to death. The average life expectancy at that time was thirty-five, and almost two-thirds of all children died before they reached four years old. Donne's father died when he was four. His brother, in prison for harboring a Catholic priest, died of a fever when Donne was twenty-one. When he was forty-five, his wife died while giving birth to their twelfth child. By this time, only seven of his twelve children were alive.

Form and Meaning

In a sonnet, it is difficult to separate the meaning of the poem from its structure. The form constrains the poet to a certain rhyme scheme and logical structure, even dictating the number of syllables and lines. In spite of this, or maybe because of this, Donne is able to pack a lot into these few, short lines. This section will be dense with new terminology, but working through the first question at the end of the chapter will help you break it down into parts so you will understand the structure of the poem more fully.

A sonnet has fourteen lines with a specific rhyme scheme. Each set of two lines, called a couplet, functions together to add meaning to the poem. The second line can be used to reinforce or restate the first line, or it can provide a contrast to what was stated in the first line. Donne uses both throughout.

Sonnets also have a specific meter, named for the number of beats (stressed syllables) per line. Most sonnets are written in iambic pentameter. An iamb is a unit of one unaccented syllable followed by an accented syllable. The root of pentameter is *penta,* which means "five." So there are five feet/ten syllables in a line written in perfect iambic pentameter. Iambic pentameter is popular in literature that is meant to be read aloud because about ten syllables is where humans would naturally take a breath. However, poets don't always follow the rules. The most famous line of what should be iambic pentameter has an extra syllable, Shakespeare's "To **be** or **not** to **be**, that **is** the **ques**tion."

Donne is not very consistent with his meter in this poem, either. He doesn't hit true iambic pentameter until line 2. The accents don't fall naturally on every second syllable until line 4, "Die **not**, poor **Death**, nor **yet** canst **thou** kill **me**." Line 1 has only nine syllables and although lines 2 and 3 have ten syllables, the accent does not naturally fall on those second syllables. Other poets in this book, such as Emily Dickinson, use perfect iambs, making it much easier to fall into the rhythm of the poem. The chapter on Dickinson has more about meter and feet.

John Donne

Donne wrote a type of sonnet called a Petrarchan (Italian) sonnet. This type of sonnet, named after the fourteenth-century Italian scholar and poet Petrarch, typically presents a logical argument of some kind. It can be broken down into two parts. The first part, lines 1 to 8, forms a proposition that describes the problem. This is sometimes called the argument. The second part, lines 9 to 14, poses a resolution to the problem. In this case, lines 9 to 12 intensify the argument through accusations leading up to the final resolution.

These groupings have formal names. The first eight lines are called an octave, which is further divided into two sets of four lines, called quatrains. Lines 9 to 14 form a sestet, which is really two sets of three lines, called tercets. Line 9 is key in this type of sonnet because that is where the argument shifts or turns. Sometimes the shift is dramatic, as in a U-turn. Other times it is a slight shift. In this poem, the intensity of the attack is what changes.

This division of parts is also reflected in the rhyme scheme. The first eight lines have a rhyme scheme of *abba abba*. Lines 9 to 14 follow a different pattern of *cddcae*. The last couplet is an unusual finish for a sonnet, however, it serves to emphasize the final rebuke of "Death, thou shalt die."

The Argument: Death Is Not Who He Thinks He Is

As the last section was dense with new terminology, these next few sections will be dense with poetic devices and meaning. Sonnets, because of their fourteen-line limitation, are dense to begin with. Donne took it to the next level by including wit, sarcasm, religious references, and allusions to things outside the poem. The structure, content, and poetic devices form a tapestry of meaning. To break it down, it helps to analyze the poem couplet by couplet.

The interweaving starts in the first couplet. Right off, Donne uses five poetic devices and introduces the theme of the poem. The first three poetic devices are related. The first poetic device is personification, where an unidentified speaker addresses death directly, saying "Death, be not proud." Personification, when used throughout a work as it is here, is a type of extended metaphor. Death is addressed as a person and then promptly insulted as a person starting in line 2 with "for thou art not so." In poetry, this kind of elaborate comparison is called a conceit.

The fourth poetic device, called apostrophe, is when someone or something is addressed that is not physically there. The fifth device Donne uses is irony, addressing death as if it is living. The theme is stated right up front: Death has a serious misconception about itself, namely that it is neither mighty nor dreadful. This theme will be expanded and the insults intensified throughout the poem. The final couplet delivers the knockout punch, putting death in its place.

Lines 3 and 4 continue the argument and the insults. As mentioned earlier, the second line of a couplet serves to either further develop the first line or provide a contrast to it. Line 3 states how death thinks of itself. In contrast, line 4 states what is really the case. The phrase "poor Death" drips with sarcasm. Death thinks he has power to conquer, but the speaker says that is not true—that people don't really die.

At this point, it is helpful to know that the references to death having no power are rooted in the Christian belief that once people die, they face judgment and then go to heaven or hell accordingly.

It is also helpful to know how Donne, the Metaphysical poet, viewed death. According to Professor Bibhudutt Dash, Donne believed that "death serves as a conduit, a medium of transporting the dead to the higher, nobler realms."[2]

It comes as no surprise then in this poem that Donne assumes a heavenly end, evidenced by the references to one's end being good. For example, in line 5, the speaker compares death to rest and sleep, stating they are but "pictures" of death. The Bible includes references to death as sleep and mentions times when people will wake from this sleep.

Line 6 draws on more biblical references. The Bible refers to sleep as pleasant and states that the sleep of the laborer is sweet. From this, the speaker surmises that sleep brings "much pleasure." He then draws the conclusion that if sleep is so great, death must be even better, "then from thee much more must flow." Another blow to death's ego.

Lines 7 and 8 finish the initial argument by implying that death is so pleasurable, people are eager to embrace it. "Soonest" means young, indicating that young men are willing to die because death is not scary, rather it is a "rest of their bones" and their "soul's delivery." Donne uses another poetic device here called a synecdoche. This is where one part of something stands for the whole of it. "Bones," a part, refers to the whole body. He also introduces ambiguity with the phrase "soul's delivery." Delivery can have several meanings here. It can mean the act of being delivered, as in a package. It can also refer to deliverance from sin. A third meaning lies in the idea of a baby being delivered. In this case, it would be the biblical idea of new birth into eternal life where death no longer exists.

The Attack: Death Is Powerless

In Petrarchan sonnets, line 9 is the pivotal point where the argument shifts in a new direction leading up to the conclusion, usually stated in the last two lines. The first eight lines present the argument that death is not scary. Rather, it is pleasurable, something to look forward to. Lines 9 to 14 make an even stronger argument. Not only is death not scary, it is powerless. Beginning with line 9, the assault turns into a character assassination. Lines 9 and 10 contain more personification. Death is referred to as a "slave." Slaves are not in control; they are under the control of their masters. In this case, "fate, chance, kings, and desperate men" are all masters of death. Not only is death a lowly creature, but line 10 argues that it dwells with other outcasts (personification again) such as "poison, war, and sickness."

Lines 11 and 12 form another contrast. Line 11 points out that "poppy or charms can make us sleep as well." A poppy is a drug that induces sleep (think of Dorothy and her friends in *The Wizard of Oz*). "Charms" refer to spells cast to get the same effect. In line 12, the speaker is back to insults. He concludes that if poppies and charms are "better than thy stroke," death has no reason to swell with pride. "Stroke" holds some ambiguity as it could mean striking, as with a weapon, or petting, as in a caress. Either meaning could work here.

The Resolution: A Paradox

The last couplet in a sonnet often presents a surprise ending. Up to this point, the speaker has been talking about falling asleep in death. In line 13, he delivers his final punch: Death is only "One short sleep past," then "we wake eternally." So not only is death powerless, it is not permanent. Waking in eternity again brings to mind the new birth, this time in a place where "death shall be no more."

As the poem began with an apostrophe, it finishes with one also. The speaker, forcefully it seems, confronts death with the words, "Death, thou shalt die." This statement represents a classic metaphysical ending, encompassing a seeming contradiction using irony. Death is already dead so it cannot die, yet it must if it does not exist in eternity.

Further Study Questions

1. Based on the information in the section "Form and Meaning," draw the structure of this Italian sonnet. Print a copy of the poem with at least 2-inch margins on each side. On the left, number the lines 1 to 14. At the end of each line, note the rhyme scheme. On the right side of the page, use brackets to note the octave, quatrains, sestet, tercets, and the turn. On the left, note whether the second line of each couplet is a restatement of the first line or a contrast to it.

2. List out all the reasons the speaker gives that death should not be proud. Which argument do you think is most effective? Why?

3. Alliteration occurs when words close together in a poem begin with the same sound or letters. Donne uses alliteration in at least half of the lines in the poem. Using a copy of the poem, circle all instances of alliteration in each line.

4. Because Donne was a Christian, he wrestled with biblical explanations of life after death. There is an underlying assumption that good people go to heaven when they die and bad ones don't. Would the conflict between faith and fear be more pronounced or less pronounced if this poem were written from the perspective of someone who believed in something else, such as reincarnation, or was atheist?

5. Write your own sonnet about death based on what you believe happens after you die. You can rewrite this poem as an insult to death using modern terminology and metaphors, or you can come up with your own form and style.

2

"We Are Seven"
William Wordsworth
(1770-1850)

Whoever said you cannot win an argument with a child was right, especially when it involves a truth that the child has lived out versus an adult's theory of how things should be. This conflict forms the basis of the poem, "We Are Seven." An adult engages an eight-year-old child in a discussion about death. More specifically, the discussion is about how to account for the dead when numbering siblings. The adult is astonished when the child insists on numbering her dead siblings as part of her family. In the end, the question is never fully resolved between the two, leaving the reader to decide.

We Are Seven

—A simple child,
That lightly draws its breath,
And feels its life in every limb,
What should it know of death?

I met a little cottage girl:
She was eight years old, she said;
Her hair was thick with many a curl
That clustered round her head.

She had a rustic, woodland air,
And she was wildly clad;
Her eyes were fair, and very fair;
—Her beauty made me glad.

"Sisters and brothers, little maid,
How many may you be?"
"How many? Seven in all," she said,
And wondering looked at me.

"And where are they? I pray you tell."
She answered, "Seven are we;
And two of us at Conway dwell,
And two are gone to sea.

"Two of us in the church-yard lie,
My sister and my brother;
And in the church-yard cottage, I
Dwell near them with my mother."

"You say that two at Conway dwell,
And two are gone to sea,
Yet ye are seven! — I pray you tell,
Sweet maid, how this may be."

Then did the little maid reply,
"Seven boys and girls are we;
Two of us in the church-yard lie,
Beneath the church-yard tree."

"You run about, my little maid,
Your limbs they are alive;
If two are in the church-yard laid,
Then ye are only five."

"Their graves are green, they may be seen,"
The little maid replied,
"Twelve steps or more from my mother's door,
And they are side by side.

"My stockings there I often knit,
My kerchief there I hem;
And there upon the ground I sit,
And sing a song to them.

"And often after sunset, sir,
When it is light and fair,
I take my little porringer,
And eat my supper there.

"The first that died was sister Jane;
In bed she moaning lay,
Till God released her of her pain;
And then she went away.

"So in the church-yard she was laid;
And, when the grass was dry,
Together round her grave we played,
My brother John and I.

"And when the ground was white with snow,
And I could run and slide,
My brother John was forced to go,
And he lies by her side."

"How many are you, then," said I,
"If they two are in heaven?"
Quick was the little maid's reply,
"O master! we are seven."

"But they are dead; those two are dead!
Their spirits are in heaven!"
'Twas throwing words away; for still
The little maid would have her will,
And say, "Nay, we are seven!"

Laying the Foundation

This poem is based on a real conversation that William Wordsworth had with a young girl. Wordsworth writes in his notes to this poem, "The little girl who is the heroine, I met within the area of Goodrich Castle in the year 1793. ... [I]n the spring of 1841, I revisited Goodrich Castle, not having seen that part of the Wye since I met the little girl there in 1793. It would have given me greater pleasure to have found in the neighbouring hamlet traces of one who had interested me so much, but that was impossible, as unfortunately I did not even know her name."[1]

The conversation made such an impact that several years later he composed a poem encapsulating the ideas. These ideas became themes that echoed throughout his life's work, from writing poems as a young idealist witnessing the French Revolution to becoming the Poet Laureate of England at the end of his life.

Even though Wordsworth was only twenty-eight years old when he wrote this poem, this early sample of his writing includes several themes found throughout the poet's work: nature, memory, and mortality. For example, nature shows itself in the description of the "little maid" as having a "rustic, woodland air" and being "wildly clad." She represents nature, instinct, and imagination. The questioner, on the other hand, represents reason. His response to her is the same after each exchange, "How many are you?" fully

Creating the Romantic Movement

Wordsworth, along with Samuel Taylor Coleridge, launched the Romantic Age in English literature with the publication of their book, *Lyrical Ballads*, in 1798. The Romantic Age was both a reaction to the previous age, the Enlightenment, and a reflection of the times, the Industrial Revolution. Literature of the previous age embodied reason, logic, and literary artifice—lofty language and formal structures. By contrast, the Romantic poets used straightforward language to explore emotions, instinct, imagination, and spirituality, often using the lyric form of poetry as in this poem.

They were known as "the nature poets," embracing the beauty of nature and the simplicity of country life. The latter is likely a reaction to the Industrial Age, a time when people migrated from the country into cities to work in the factories. In Romantic literature, this pull toward the natural was to counterbalance the ongoing separation of man from nature. They believed that man and nature should come back together for man to experience wholeness and a return to his natural state.

expecting her to realize that death is the end of existence, therefore they should not be counted.

A second theme, memory, plays an integral part in this poem. It is the girl's memories of her siblings that keep them alive. She remembers when they lived and how they died. She remembers playing with them when alive and playing near them once they are laid to rest. Wordsworth explores the theme of mortality through the conversation. He juxtaposes the ideas of the adult with the convictions of the child. To the adult, the siblings are dead. To the child, they are alive. His underlying question is, "When does mortality end—with cessation of life or cessation of memories of that life?" He leaves the question open.

The Story

Wordsworth wrote this poem from the bottom up. He states, "[In regard] to *We are Seven,* . . . I composed it while walking in the grove at Alfoxden. My friends will not deem it too trifling to relate, that while walking to and fro I composed the last stanza first, having begun with the last line. When it was all but finished, I came in and recited it to Mr. Coleridge and my sister, and said, 'A prefatory stanza must be added, and I should sit down to our little tea-meal with greater pleasure if my task was finished.' I mentioned in substance what I wished to be expressed, and Coleridge immediately threw off the stanza."[2]

Collaboration with Samuel Taylor Coleridge

Wordsworth and Coleridge shared ideas on their poems during their treks around the area where they lived. At Wordsworth's request, Coleridge contributed the first stanza to "We Are Seven." The first line originally had what they considered a humorous tribute to a mutual friend nicknamed Jem and read "A little child, dear brother Jem." Thinking it might offend their friend, Wordsworth dropped the "dear brother Jem" part. It was not replaced with anything else, so the first line of the poem as published has only two beats.

They began to collaborate on a work that became "The Rime of the Ancient Mariner," but Wordsworth dropped out of the process shortly after it was begun. He said, "As we endeavored to proceed conjointly . . . our respective manners proved so widely different that it would have been quite presumptuous in me to do anything but separate from an undertaking upon which I could only have been a clog."[3]

The first stanza achieves Wordsworth's goal of providing an introduction. The reader gets a sense of standing back and watching a child at play. The child is full of "breath" and "life." Then comes the abrupt question: "What should it know of death?" The speaker takes on the air of superior knowledge, setting the stage for the discussion to come.

The next two stanzas provide a more detailed description of the child, an eight-year-old girl at play. There is still the sense of watching, but the reader is drawn to the girl along with the speaker. In lines 7 and 8, he gives a physical description of the girl's hair being "thick with many a curl" and "clustered round her head." Then he switches to describing her as a thing of nature with a "rustic, woodland air," and being "wildly clad." In line 11, he goes back to a physical description of her eyes. He sums up his emotions upon watching this scene by saying, "Her beauty made me glad."

Wordsworth adeptly switches from the physical to the natural, then back to the physical, and ends with the emotional. This interplay is important to the Romantic's way of thinking. Here, the girl is grounded in nature, evoking pleasant emotions in the observer. This is the antithesis of what will soon become obvious—that the adult is grounded in logic and reason.

The conversation begins in line 13. The speaker asks the girl an ordinary question about how many siblings she has. She answers, "Seven in all," but "wondering" looks at the speaker as if it were an odd question. In line 17, he continues the conversation by asking where they are. The girl restates the number seven, and then explains that four of them have moved away, two of them are buried in the churchyard, and she lives with her mother in the churchyard cottage.

A little back and forth continues through line 24 as the speaker questions her accounting for the dead as if they were alive. In lines 25 to 28, the speaker gently tries to get her to see that there are the four that have moved away and her, so how can she say they are seven? In lines 29 to 32, she simply adds the two who have died to the four he mentions. He pushes a little harder in lines 33 to 36, comparing her being alive to them being dead.

William Wordsworth

At this point, she takes it upon herself to explain. The next three stanzas detail her physical interactions with her dead siblings. She describes their graves and where they are located in proximity to her house. She tells how she visits the graves and knits stockings, hems kerchiefs, sings to them, and eats supper there. In her mind, they are alive as she still has a relationship with them. The stranger must not have looked too convinced because she goes on for another three stanzas describing the relationship she had with them before they died. She remembers her sister Jane was sick in bed and "God released her of her pain." She was buried, and the girl would play around her grave with their brother John.

When winter came, John was "forced to go," indicating a sudden, unexpected death. This further explanation shows that not only does she have a relationship with them in their graves, but they also stay alive in her memories.

The speaker, thinking the girl can now account for the deaths logically—as he would—after realizing that she still plays when her brother and sister do not, asks how many are you "If they two are in heaven?" She seems even more adamant in her answer, "O master! We are seven." The exclamation point emphasizes that instead of being persuaded to his point of view, she is now even more certain of hers. In lines 65 and 66, he tries to convince her one last time that because their spirits are in heaven and not on earth, she cannot count them. The exclamation point accompanying his words shows that he is equally convinced of his accounting being right. At last, he gives in realizing, "'Twas throwing words away." The adult, representing reason, has lost the argument to the child, who represents the newly emerging Romantic ideal of emotional experience over reason.

Poetry for the Common Man

Wordsworth believed in treating all men equal, from the lowest beggar to the highest in society. According to Arthur Bell and Bernard Grebanier, this came in part from "the theories developed in France establishing the principles of Liberty, Fraternity and Equality."[4] Most of the Romantic poets spent time in France as the French Revolution was forming and embraced these principles. The French Revolution (1789–1799) had many of the same ideas as the American Revolution (1775–1783). When France's monarchy fell, the new government was based on principles similar to those of the then-new United States— equality and inalienable rights. Even though most of the Romantic poets lost faith in the movement once Napoleon took over in France, they kept their ideals of equality and liberty.

As part of this belief in equality, Wordsworth wanted his poetry to be accessible to all, not just the highly educated. He used the lyric form of poetry that tells a story and straightforward language to tell it. So, instead of requiring years of studying English literature to catch all the allusions in his poems, he confined the ideas to the present and related them to the natural world that everyone understood.

This poem is written in stanzas of four lines, except the last stanza, which has five. With the exception of the first line, the odd-numbered lines have four feet, and the even have three. This rhythm was common to hymns, so that would have made it a familiar cadence for reading. Also, the rhyme scheme is regular, for the most part. For a majority of the stanzas, it is *abab*. Some of the feet vary in the number of unstressed syllables, but the poem is still accessible.

Though he rejected lofty language, Wordsworth freely used poetic devices. For example, he used alliteration in every stanza. Sometimes, as in line 3, the words are separated, as in "life" and "limb." Other times, as in lines 7 and 8, the words will be together as in "Her hair" and "her head." He used repetition of words or phrases such as "seven," "in the church-yard," and "how many?" to punctuate their meaning and raise their importance. For example, "church-yard" appears in lines 21, 23, 31, 32, 35, and 53, and "seven" appears in lines 15, 18, 27, 30, 64, and 69.

In the last stanza, Wordsworth throws away his own structure and adds an extra line. The rhyme scheme on the last stanza is *abccb*. The jarring nature of the stanza reflects the jarring conclusion the speaker has reached. It is almost as if he is shaking his head to clear it, while repeating these lines to himself.

When Is the End the End?

Throughout, the poem is a play between life and death. The speaker describes the girl who is alive with words that show movement, activity, and life. The dead siblings are only described as being in the churchyard and lying side by side. The little girl makes the same distinction when she describes her time with her siblings before and after their deaths, yet she still insists on counting them as alive. Wordsworth does not resolve the conflict but leaves the reader to decide.

Further Study Questions

1. Print a copy of the poem and mark all the instances of alliteration. Does Wordsworth use those devices more frequently with one speaker than the other? What effect does this have?

2. Wordsworth sometimes uses more than one type of foot in a line. Identify where this occurs. Do you think it adds to the poem, or is it just sloppy writing?

3. Does the speaker ever change his method of persuasion? It is effective? What is the speaker's realization at the end of the poem?

4. Does the age of the girl matter? Would the story be as believable if the child were a teenager? Do you think she would have the same relationship with her dead siblings if she didn't live only twelve steps from their graves?

5. A friend of Wordsworth's suggested he remove this poem from his first book before it was published in order to save his reputation. Wordsworth insisted it stay. Compare this poem to "Lines Written a Few Miles Above Tintern Abbey." Why do you think his friend would say "We Are Seven" could somehow tarnish his reputation?

3

"No Coward Soul Is Mine"
Emily Brontë
(1818-1848)

Have you ever been captivated and carried away by the rhetoric of a great speech? This poem does just that. It is a poem of passion, persuasion, and power. The poet displays a passion for God, gives reasons to believe, and compares the power of God to the powerlessness of death. Surprisingly, this poem was not written for publication. The poet was a private person and wrote it as a private statement of faith. It was the last poem she wrote.

"An Icon to Tortured Genius"

Emily Brontë lived in Haworth, in Yorkshire, England. Her father was curate, or priest, of the parish of Haworth. He was a poet and writer as well. Brontë had four sisters and a brother. Her mother died when she was three, and two of her older sisters died during Emily's childhood when they became ill while away at school. These deaths had a profound effect upon the surviving siblings, especially Emily.

In all of her stories, the main characters are orphans or have absent parents. She and her three surviving siblings, Charlotte, Branwell, and Anne, were not sent off to school but stayed at home and were educated by her father and her mother's sister.

The siblings collaborated on a fantasy series that began when they were young. As they matured, Anne and Emily broke off to write a competing fantasy, while Charlotte and Branwell continued with the original. It is within this context of family tragedy and great imagination that the three Brontë sisters developed into famous writers.

Emily Brontë is best known for her one novel, *Wuthering Heights*, a passionate story about doomed love. The novel plumbed the depths of depravity of human relationships, showing passion at its worst. Passion seems to be the personal signature on her work. Biographer C. D. Merriman writes, "Emily has been characterised to mythic proportions as deeply spiritual, free-spirited and reclusive as well as intensely creative and passionate, an icon to tortured genius."[1]

Similarities to Emily Dickinson

There are remarkable similarities between the lives of Brontë and Emily Dickinson. They lived at approximately the same time but in two different countries. They both had religious upbringings that profoundly affected their lives and their poetry. They both rejected the traditional practice of religion and replaced it with an appreciation of nature instead. Both lived reclusive lives and wrote poetry for themselves, not for publication. Both had siblings who insisted their work be published. Dickinson was aware of Brontë's work. Dickinson requested that Brontë's "No Coward Soul Is Mine" be read at her funeral. For differences between the two, see the sidebar in the chapter on Dickinson.

The poem "No Coward Soul Is Mine" is one of her most famous poems, and many of those traits shine through. Brontë's free-spiritedness appears in her unconventional approach to both her religion and her writing. She rejected organized religion, preferring a personal approach to faith. Her poems broke tradition in both form and content. Her literary career was cut short when she died at the age of thirty from consumption, now known as tuberculosis.

No Coward Soul Is Mine

No coward soul is mine,
No trembler in the world's storm-troubled sphere:
I see Heaven's glories shine,
And faith shines equal, arming me from fear.

O God within my breast.
Almighty, ever-present Deity!
Life — that in me has rest,
As I — Undying Life — have power in Thee!

Vain are the thousand creeds
That move mens hearts: unutterably vain;
Worthless as withered weeds,
Or idlest froth amid the boundless main,

To waken doubt in one
Holding so fast by Thine infinity;
So surely anchored on
The steadfast rock of immortality.

With wide-embracing love
Thy Spirit animates eternal years,
Pervades and broods above,
Changes, sustains, dissolves, creates, and rears.

Though earth and moon were gone,
And suns and universes ceased to be,
And Thou wert left alone,
Every Existence would exist in Thee.

There is not room for Death,
Nor atom that his might could render void:
Thou — Thou art Being and Breath,
And what Thou art may never be destroyed.

Unwavering Faith

"No Coward Soul Is Mine" serves as both a statement of faith and a challenge to the reader to examine his or her beliefs. Brontë was a private person and wrote for herself, not for the masses. She states her thoughts directly with

Emily Brontë

uncomplicated language. The poem alludes to both the Bible and the Romantic Era idea of the universal intertwining of God and nature. The poem is first interpreted in its biblical context and then in its Romantic Era context.

The poem consists of seven four-line stanzas with alternating lines of iambic trimeter and iambic pentameter. (See chapters on Emily Dickinson and John Donne for more information on meter.) In general, the trimeter lines make a statement that the pentameter lines clarify, extend, or expound upon. Because of the depth of feeling involved and what is known of Brontë's life, the speaker in the poem is assumed to be the poet. The first two stanzas comprise her statement of faith, the next two serve as a call to examine beliefs, and the last three stanzas give reasons to believe and further statements of faith. To build her case, Brontë uses a variety of metaphors for both God and death throughout the poem to fine-tune and intensify their meaning.

Statement of Faith

The poem opens with a strong statement that "the world's storm-troubled sphere" holds no fear for the speaker. In lines 3 and 4, she immediately follows up with a reason why. She has seen "Heaven's glories shine," and states that her "Faith shines equal." In other words, what she believes and what she has seen as proof of those beliefs give her faith and form a shield about her, "arming me from Fear."

This phrase is an allusion to the shield of faith, part of a Christian's armor in spiritual warfare.[2]

This stanza introduces one of the themes present throughout the work, the contrast of light and life to darkness and death. Storms cover the sky with dark clouds and often incite fear, yet the speaker sees "Heaven's glories shine," protecting her from fear during the storm. In line 4, Brontë uses the poetic device of personification to strengthen the emotional impact of "Fear" by capitalizing it.

The second stanza delves into her relationship with God where "God is within my breast" and she has "power in Thee." This might seem weird, but it is an allusion to a Christian doctrine that states the moment a person believes, he is sealed with a deposit of the Holy Spirit, who then guides the person from the inside out through life's moral landscape.[3] That deposit also comes with a guarantee that the true believer cannot be taken from the hand of God and will end up in heaven for eternity as a result.[4] This doctrine forms the bedrock of her faith, and the remainder of a biblical interpretation of the poem flows from it.

A Call for Self-Examination

By the third stanza, it is obvious the speaker has strong beliefs. She now contrasts those with "the thousand creeds/ That move men's hearts." She considers them "vain," "worthless," and "idlest froth." Brontë bucked convention in several areas in life. Two of them show up in the third and fourth stanzas. She rebelled against organized religion of all types, referred to here as "the thousand creeds." She preferred, instead, to focus on her personal relationship with God rather than go through the formulaic church services of her day. Critics have variously described her as an atheist, agnostic, or Christian mystic, making her statements of faith surprising.[5] But her rejection of formal religion was partially a reaction to her sisters' religious experience. They constantly struggled with sin in accordance with the church's teaching that not following the church's rules meant certain damnation. Emily had no such qualms.

In the fourth stanza, she continues her thought that these vanities are "unable to awaken doubt in one/Holding so fast by Thine infinity." Here, she breaks poetic convention. The thoughts in the fourth stanza are incomplete without the stanza just before. Traditionally and stylistically, poets completed one thought or made one point in each stanza. The thought that spans lines 9 to 16 is that men's practice of religion and their various beliefs hold no sway over her because she is "So surely anchored on/The steadfast rock of immortality."

In the third stanza, it seems she is rejecting men's creeds, and she is. But her purpose in stating that is to build up to the argument in the fourth stanza that those creeds have no power to make her doubt. Her faith is not in the rituals of religion but in her relationship with God. She is subtly implying that others should examine their beliefs to see if their faith is in a powerful God or a powerless ideology. At the time this was written, her father was curate of an Anglican Church. Dissenters, the Protestants who separated from the Church of England, were challenging churches all across England. Brontë was not distracted from her beliefs by these various interpretations of the practice of religion.

Brontë uses the poetic device of alliteration liberally throughout this section. Sometimes it is visually obvious, such as "Worthless as withered weeds" in line 11. Other times the alliteration is hidden due to different ways to spell a sound, as in "waken" and "one" in line 13. The visual appearance of words can be important in poetry. Notice in the fourth stanza that none of the lines rhyme, but they look like they should. For example, "one" and "on" look similar but do not rhyme. "Infinity" and "immortality" look like they should but don't quite rhyme, either. This is called a visual rhyme, as opposed to audible rhyme. Brontë reverts to visual rhyme so she can get her points across within the confines of her meter. She uses this technique one other time in lines 21 and 23.

Reasons to Believe

In the fifth stanza, the speaker transitions back to speaking about how God operates on earth through "Thy Spirit." She starts by mentioning a "wide-embracing love" in line

17. Although taught that only a select few would get into heaven, Brontë believed in a more liberal God who would welcome those who believed, especially those who had suffered in this life. In the poem, this "wide-embracing love" comes through "Thy Spirit" who actively watches over humanity, who "animates eternal years,/Pervades and broods above." Not only does this eternal being watch from above, he dips down into the affairs of men and "Changes, sustains, dissolves, creates and rears." This activity of God is the proof she provides for those who argue over their creeds and her invitation to others to believe as she does.

After zooming down to earth, the speaker goes back to the lofty heights of heaven and beyond, to "universes." She states that though all creation, identified as "earth," "moon," "suns," and "universes," ceased to be and only God was left, everything would still "exist in Thee." This cessation of creation refers to the end times of the Bible, when God destroys what has been and creates a new heaven and a new earth. The speaker believes that even when that happens, her eternal soul will not be destroyed but will still be in eternity with God.

The last stanza returns the reader to earth. Recall in the first stanza how the speaker's soul would not cower before the world's troubles. Here, she confronts the ultimate fear— fear of death. In her world filled with a passionate faith in a powerful God, "There is not room for Death." Death is so powerless it cannot alter one atom of God's creation.

The last two lines serve as her ultimate realization, that "Thou art Being and Breath/And what Thou art may never be destroyed." Whether in the midst of a storm-tossed existence or facing the ultimate destroyer—death—she has no fear because of her faith in an eternal life with God in heaven, stated as "what Thou art may never be destroyed." The argument ends here. "No coward soul is mine" even when she faces death because the proof of God's promises she has seen in this life leads her to believe in the promise of eternal life.

An Alternate Interpretation

The interpretation laid out so far stems from a traditional view of Christianity. Another view can be taken and even intertwined with the one above, as Brontë's work was a product of both Christianity and Romanticism. The English Romantic period was at its peak near the end of Brontë's life. It had grown out of and as a push back against the Age of Enlightenment, a movement to reform society through reason rather than religion and to promote science and rational intellect over tradition and emotion.

In contrast, proponents of the Romantic Era elevated strong emotion and untamed nature. They played with the idea of a life force in nature that encompassed God and man and extended into life after death somewhere in the universe. Art became an escape from the effects of the Industrial Age, such as populations becoming concentrated in cities and the move from the natural to the mechanical. Artists embraced both the good in human nature and its dark side.

Brontë explored the darker side of human nature in her only novel, *Wuthering Heights*. Within that longer work, she developed characters that represented all she saw wrong with society, from narrow religion to the British class system. She explored a system of heaven and hell that included a sort of twisted redemption through mental and physical suffering on earth and led to the destruction of lives. In contrast, this poem explores the constructive side of strong human emotion, focusing on being one with the natural world and experiencing the presence of God on earth. In *Wuthering Heights*, she focuses on life as a type of hell on earth. In this poem, she focuses on a taste of heaven on earth.

In the first stanza, the speaker contrasts the "world's storm-troubled sphere" with "Heaven's glories." She sets up her argument for a faith that overcomes fear of life's troubles, one of those being death, which she comes to in the last stanza. The argument builds in lines 5 to 8, where "God within my breast" gives her "power in Thee!" She intertwines the creator with the created, the divine with the natural. The power of the divine sustains the natural in times of trouble, freeing her from fear. "Undying Life" in line 8 is a reference to the Romantic's idea of a life force running throughout the universe. This force serves as the connection between God and man.

The next section serves as a rebuttal of the Age of Reason. People vainly use their intellect, "the thousand creeds," to elicit an emotional response "[t]hat move[s] men's hearts." The intellectual approach is "worthless as withered weeds" to combat her faith, "To waken doubt" in her. Her faith is not one of words; it is based on strong emotions and action, "holding so fast" and attaching herself to the "steadfast rock of immortality."

In the fifth stanza, the speaker goes back to showing how God invades men's lives. The Spirit "pervades and broods" and "Changes, sustains, dissolves, creates and rears" in order to direct the lives of men through their natural circumstances. This fusion of man and God with nature as mediator is so complete that even if nature in all its "universes" were to disappear, man would still exist with God through the universal life force: "Every Existence would exist in Thee."

The conclusion in the last stanza is that death is of no consequence, and therefore nothing to be feared. It is simply an experience of nature, a change from one type of being on earth to another type in eternity.

With either interpretation, the poem displays an exquisite irony. Brontë uses a logical argument, which would fall under the Age of Reason, to persuade readers of the sincerity of her emotion, a tenant of Romanticism. Like God and nature, reason and emotion are separate entities, but they work together to form a comprehensive whole.

Further Study Questions

1. Make a list of all the imagery referring to the concepts of light and darkness in the poem. Does Brontë treat one differently than the other?

2. Look up the definition of each of the words used in lines 19 and 20. What do you think Brontë is trying to communicate by choosing those specific words?

3. What does Brontë mean in line 26 when she says, "Nor atom that his might could render void"?

4. What is Brontë's view of the afterlife in this poem?

5. Do you lean more toward the biblical interpretation or the Romantic Era one? Why?

4

"Good-by" Ralph Waldo Emerson
(1803-1882)

In Christian theology, there is a doctrine of dying to self in order to gain in the next world. "Dying to self" means putting the will of God and needs of others before your own. In this poem, Ralph Waldo Emerson espouses a doctrine of dying to the world to realize the self. His is an interesting take on the idea because Emerson was a trained minister who would have been familiar with that Christian doctrine. Whereas the theological response is supposedly based on a superior love of humankind, Emerson's response was based on the intellectual superiority of that special class of people known as poets, who he believed were to be a representative whole summing up the parts of the society in which they lived. He was quite an outlier during his lifetime, often coming up with ideas that were outside the accepted way of thinking. Many of his teachings created controversy in both intellectual and religious circles, even while his popularity as an essayist and lecturer grew.

Emerson and Transcendentalism

Ralph Waldo Emerson was the chief representative of the transcendental movement, a philosophical, religious, and literary movement that began in America. Proponents of the movement embraced the rejection of scientific rationalism, preferring instead to believe that everything in nature was supreme and each part was a microcosm, or miniature representation, of the universe. In his works, Emerson did not separate matter (science) and the soul (religion) but thought of them as united. However, he did wrestle with how they fit together.

Emerson's father died before he turned eight. At fourteen, he entered Harvard College, graduating in the middle of his class. He became schoolmaster and attended Harvard Divinity School, accepting a position as junior pastor at Boston's Second Church. He married young but lost his wife to tuberculosis within two years. At this point, he began doubting his beliefs and the form of church worship. This internal conflict spawned his journey to determine how the mind and matter fit together. Was the mind matter or spirit? Are thoughts a reaction to the senses or a reflection of the divine? What is the interplay between

Emerson Sounds the Call

In his essay "The Poet," Emerson called for a uniquely American poetic voice to rise up and capture the essence of America with its rugged individualism and rapid westward expansion. He felt the poet had a unique place in culture and should capture the ideals for the masses. He states, "The breadth of the problem is great, for the poet is representative. He stands among partial men for the complete man, and apprises us not of his wealth, but of the commonwealth."[1]

Walt Whitman's *Leaves of Grass* was a direct response to this call. Henry David Thoreau was another friend and disciple of Emerson's who lived out his creed.

God, man, and nature? He spent his life exploring these ideas. In his early days, it took on a romantic air, but in his later years, he became more practical.

His thoughts and beliefs meshed well with the emerging Romantic period that was just beginning in Britain. After Emerson left the ministry, he took a trip to Europe where he met Samuel Taylor Coleridge and Thomas Carlyle, two influential leaders of the Romantic movement in Britain. He learned through his friendship with them, especially Carlyle with whom he corresponded for thirty-eight years.

Good-by

Good-by, proud world, I'm going home,
Thou'rt not my friend, and I'm not thine;
Long through thy weary crowds I roam;
A river-ark on the ocean brine,
Long I've been tossed like the driven foam,
But now, proud world, I'm going home.

Good-by to Flattery's fawning face,
To Grandeur, with his wise grimace,
To upstart Wealth's averted eye,
To supple Office low and high,
To crowded halls, to court, and street,
To frozen hearts, and hasting feet,
To those who go, and those who come,
Good-by, proud world, I'm going home.

I'm going to my own hearth-stone
Bosomed in yon green hills, alone,
A secret nook in a pleasant land,
Whose groves the frolic fairies planned;
Where arches green the livelong day
Echo the blackbird's roundelay,
And vulgar feet have never trod
A spot that is sacred to thought and God.

Oh, when I am safe in my sylvan home,
I tread on the pride of Greece and Rome;
And when I am stretched beneath the pines
Where the evening star so holy shines,
I laugh at the lore and the pride of man,
At the sophist schools, and the learned clan;
For what are they all in their high conceit,
When man in the bush with God may meet.

Becoming Dead to the World

This poem was written when Emerson was young. It reflects his idealism regarding society versus self-reliance. He promotes separation from society as a good thing and necessary for inner searching. Although not traditionally looked at this way, the poem can be interpreted as a need to become dead to the world in order to find the true self, a twist of the biblical paradox that if one gains the world, he loses his soul and vice versa.

When interpreted as such, the poem is a study in irony. The society that Emerson rejects is what allowed him to become the intellect he was—rubbing shoulders with great thinkers through travel and education. Many of the ideas he espoused were based on the ideas of his contemporaries. He may have died to the world to find himself, but then he returned to "those sophist schools" and "learned clan[s]" to share what he had found.

In Ancient Greece, the Sophists claimed to be teachers of virtue and excellence but charged for their "wisdom." The word sophist evolved to mean someone who uses an argument that deliberately misleads. Emerson may be playing with both meanings. When he returned from Europe, he became a traveling lecturer, constantly thrust into the "crowded halls" of those seeking to find themselves. In later years, he must have had some inkling of the irony. He almost did not publish this poem with his later material.

Railing Against the World

"Good-by" can be divided into two sections. In the first two stanzas, the speaker criticizes the world. Next, in the second two stanzas, he romanticizes a home tucked away in nature. There is a complete rejection of society in one; a total embrace of nature and self-realization in the other. Line 1 sets up the conflict immediately. The speaker calls the world "proud" and rejects it by stating, "I'm going home." The second line reinforces that further by pointing out there is no love lost between the two.

The speaker then launches into a general description of the world filled with weary crowds and a boat adrift on the water like a "river-ark on the ocean brine." A river-ark was a crude raft built to move goods downriver. It had no steering mechanism and was at the mercy of the wind and the current. This one ends up in the ocean brine, a mixture of salt water and fresh water that occurs where a river meets the sea. It is obviously off course and in danger of being swept out to sea. Brine is also used for pickling. The speaker could be thinking that if he stayed in the city much longer, he would be pickled with the same worldliness he leaves behind in stanza 2. Line 6 is a repeat of the sentiment in line 1, emphasizing its importance.

In the second stanza, the speaker gets specific, naming the things that disenchant him. First, he mentions "Flattery's fawning face," and "Grandeur, with his wise grimace."

Ralph Waldo Emerson

The alliteration makes the words drip with loathing. He is rejecting those who put on airs. In lines 9 and 10, he rejects the wealthy and the politicians. His mention of "upstart Wealth's averted eye" indicates a certain shame in chasing after money. His scorn does not spare those in leadership and government, referring to their "supple Office low and high," recognizing that politics is a game of compromise where you may have to be flexible with what you believe— the ultimate betrayal to a poet who works to be true to himself.

Lines 11 to 13 sum up the rest of humanity, with the "crowded halls" and "those who go, and those who come." He notes their "frozen hearts" and "hasting feet," bringing to mind the idea of people, the unthinking man, going mindlessly about the business of the material life. The speaker ends with one last thrust, a repeat of the first line of the poem.

Embracing Home

Now comes the description of home. The change in language reveals a completely different side to the speaker. What might have seemed like bitterness in the first two stanzas turns into an appreciation for nature and solitude. Right away in line 15, the change is evident. He starts by referring to his hearth-stone, indicating rest and comfort. In line 16, his home is "Bosomed in yon green hills," promoting the idea of getting back to nature. In contrast to the busyness of the city, his home stands "alone" in "A secret nook." The imagery continues in lines 17 to 20 with "pleasant land" and "groves" planned by fairies with "arches green." The whole scene is one of rest among nature, of slowing down to absorb the benefits of a natural setting.

In line 21, you see a brief flash of the revulsion he expressed in the earlier stanzas. His reference to "Vulgar feet" reveals what he thinks of those who have chased material gain. He further chastises the unworthy, calling the spot "sacred to thought and God." His sharp contrast between pursuing the "sacred" in line 22 and the "vulgar" in line 21 further reveals his disgust for that other way of life.

In the fourth stanza, the speaker arrives at his destination, which is a "safe" place in a "sylvan," or wooded, setting. In line 24, there is another quick flash of rejection of rationalism with "I tread on the pride of Greece and Rome." Greek and Roman thought, often celebrated for their advancements in science and philosophy, formed the foundation of Western civilization. They represent the collective knowledge of humankind, embodied in the literature of the preceding Age of Reason. The speaker rejects this earthly reasoning gained through "sophist schools" and being part of "the learned clan." Instead, he stretches beneath the pines and contemplates the evening star as it "so holy shines."

Being "stretched beneath the pines" could be a metaphor for death, as people were often laid to rest under a special tree on the family property. His reference to holiness in line 26 and God in line 30 adds a spiritual aspect to this last stanza. The speaker dismisses the trappings of civilization, "For what are they all in their high conceit," in effect dying to them.

Transcendentalism Defined

In an 1842 lecture, Emerson defined transcendentalism. He identified its origin in Immanuel Kant's argument that there was " . . . a very important class of ideas, or imperative forms, which did not come by experience, but through which experience was acquired; that these were intuitions of the mind itself; and [Kant] denominated them *Transcendental* forms."[2]

Emerson suggested that transcendental thought existed throughout time and showed itself in purest form when unselfish individuals displayed genius and virtue in challenging circumstances. He goes on to give examples throughout history, ending with the transcendentalists of his time: "This way of thinking, falling on Roman times, made Stoic philosophers; falling on despotic times, made patriot Catos and Brutuses; falling on superstitious times, made prophets and apostles; on popish times, made protestants and ascetic monks, preachers of Faith against the preachers of Works; on prelatical times, made Puritans and Quakers; and falling on Unitarian and commercial times, makes the peculiar shades of Idealism which we know."[3] The transcendentalists identified themselves as idealists.

When people die, it is said they go to meet their Maker. The last line alludes to the idea that he has died to the world to meet with God, but he does it here on earth, "in the bush," possibly an allusion to Moses meeting God here on earth through the burning bush on Mount Sinai.

Poetic Devices

Emerson was first a philosopher and then a poet. As a philosopher, he gave lectures and wrote essays, delivering intellectual treatises with extensive prose. As a poet, he captured his philosophy in an abbreviated form of art. The abbreviated form required him to use poetic devices to get his meaning across in few words. One of the devices he used was repetition. The word "home" is repeated at the end of lines 1, 6, 14, and 23. Repetition creates emphasis and often points to a theme in the poem. The speaker claims his true home among the natural, not the material. Another type of repetition is anaphora, repeating a word or phrase at the beginning of a line, as in lines 8 to 13. Each line emphasizes an aspect of the world he is leaving behind. The repetition of "home" and "To" gives a vague impression of sarcasm, like the speaker is taunting someone.

To fit words into a specific meter, poets often shortened words by removing syllables and replacing them with an apostrophe. This is a poetic device called elision. Emerson uses it in line 2 to shorten "Thou art" into "Thou'rt." Another common device is simile, the comparison of two things using *like, than, as,* or *seems.* Line 5 contains a simile comparing the speaker's life in the city to a raft with no direction.

Echoes of Irony

It is interesting to note that the pride he accuses the world of having he now displays about his own world. Again, this was a young Emerson. As his life progressed, he did indeed die to the idea of being part of the community but became a leader of that same community by embracing his individuality, becoming a leader of a movement and a great influence on future generations of Americans as a champion of individualism. Critic Harold Bloom states, "The whole phenomenon of American culture, on every level down to popular culture is a profoundly Emersonian affair. He has prophesied everything. . . . He is the mind of America."[4]

Further Study Questions

1. Emerson was a minister who struggled with his beliefs. He lived during a time of great change, national expansion, and growing individualism. How are these experiences reflected in the poem? Does the speaker seem to embrace them or reject them?

2. In the second stanza, Emerson gives a list of specific things the speaker rejects. How does each of these things represent civilization and worldliness?

3. Notice the language Emerson uses throughout the poem. Create a chart comparing the differences in attitude toward civilization (stanzas 1 and 2) and nature (stanzas 3 and 4).

4. Does the organization of the poem into two distinct attitudes serve to persuade the reader at all? Why or why not?

5. Which is more necessary to experience individual fulfillment, withdrawing from the world to experience self or dying to self to promote the welfare of humanity? Or are they the same thing?

5

"The Charge of the Light Brigade"
Alfred, Lord Tennyson
(1809–1892)

What happens when a superior officer gives a command that the soldiers know is stupid, wrong, or worse—one that means almost certain death? Should the soldiers follow the command or develop a new plan on their own? In the military, without a chain of command and the expectation that orders will be followed, any campaign would soon be chaos and most likely fail. The soldiers in this poem, based on a true story during the Crimean War, are faced with this situation. They are given an order that means almost certain death. Their response demonstrates the nobility of the human spirit in the face of death.

Alfred, Poet Laureate

Alfred, Lord Tennyson, became Poet Laureate of England in 1850, following the death of William Wordsworth. He was already a well-known poet at the time, and his fame grew during his forty-two years as Poet Laureate under Queen Victoria. The Poet Laureate's job was to write poetry appropriate to royal occasions or items of national interest. He had been Poet Laureate for four years when the incident in this poem took place. He read a newspaper account of the Battle of Balaclava between the British and the Russians during the Crimean War. He was so inspired by the soldiers that he wrote this poem in a few minutes. It became popular in England and was circulated among the troops.

For being written so quickly, it is amazingly well put together. Doing a quick read, the poem gives a simple snapshot of the battle: the charge into the fray, the battle, and then the retreat back to safety. However, with a closer read, something interesting starts to emerge. The rhythm of the words and even the sounds they make call to mind the sights and sounds of battle. In addition, the choice of words reflects an emotional element that runs throughout. At times, Tennyson quickly switches in and out of different points of view. All of these elements come together to make this one of the most memorable poems about the nobility and horror of war.

The News Story That Sparked Tennyson's Ideas

The Crimean War was Britain's first war that included on-the-scene reporters and photographers. It was William Howard Russell's eyewitness news report, excerpted below, that Tennyson based his work on.

- "At 11:00 our Light Cavalry Brigade rushed to the front. . . . The Russians opened on them with guns from the redoubts on the right, with volleys of musketry and rifles. They swept proudly past, glittering in the morning sun in all the pride and splendor of war. We could hardly believe the evidence of our senses. Surely that handful of men were not going to charge an army in position? . . .

- "With diminished ranks, thinned by those thirty guns, which the Russians had laid with the most deadly accuracy, with a halo of flashing steel above their heads, and with a cheer which was many a noble fellow's death cry, they flew into the smoke of the batteries . . .

- "Through the clouds of smoke we could see their sabers flashing as they rode up to the guns and dashed between them, cutting down the gunners as they stood. . . .

- "It was as much as our Heavy Cavalry Brigade could do to cover the retreat of the miserable remnants of that band of heroes as they returned to the place they had so lately quitted in all the pride of life. At 11:35 not a British soldier, except the dead and dying, was left in front of those bloody Muscovite guns . . . "[1]

The Charge of the Light Brigade

1.

Half a league, half a league,
Half a league onward,
All in the valley of Death
Rode the six hundred.
"Forward, the Light Brigade!
"Charge for the guns!" he said:
Into the valley of Death
Rode the six hundred.

2.

"Forward, the Light Brigade!"
Was there a man dismay'd?
Not tho' the soldier knew
Some one had blunder'd:
Theirs not to make reply,
Theirs not to reason why,
Theirs but to do and die:
Into the valley of Death
Rode the six hundred.

3.

Cannon to right of them,
Cannon to left of them,
Cannon in front of them
Volley'd and thunder'd;
Storm'd at with shot and shell,
Boldly they rode and well,
Into the jaws of Death,
Into the mouth of Hell
Rode the six hundred.

4.

Flash'd all their sabres bare,
Flash'd as they turn'd in air,
Sabring the gunners there,
Charging an army, while
   All the world wonder'd:
Plunged in the battery-smoke
Right thro' the line they broke;
Cossack and Russian
Reel'd from the sabre stroke
   Shatter'd and sunder'd.
Then they rode back, but not
   Not the six hundred.

5.

Cannon to right of them,
Cannon to left of them,
Cannon behind them
   Volley'd and thunder'd;
Storm'd at with shot and shell,
While horse and hero fell,
They that had fought so well
Came thro' the jaws of Death
Back from the mouth of Hell,
All that was left of them,
   Left of six hundred.

6.

When can their glory fade?
O the wild charge they made!
   All the world wondered.
Honor the charge they made,
Honor the Light Brigade,
   Noble six hundred.

The Sounds of War, the Sounds of Words

The poem is organized into six stanzas of unequal length, varying from six to twelve lines. This does not allow for a set rhyme scheme. Some lines rhyme within a stanza, but more important is Tennyson's use of repetition. His repetition of words or phrases within a line or series of lines shows emphasis and keeps the reader focused on the subject of the poem.

The meter, along with repetition, creates a distinct rhythm. The formal name for the meter is dactylic dimeter. A dactyl is a poetic foot with one stressed syllable followed by two unstressed syllables. Dimeter means each line has two feet. A poetic foot that starts with a single stressed syllable and is followed by one or more unstressed syllables is said to have a falling meter. The unstressed syllables seem to fall off, almost like an echo fading in the distance. Note throughout the poem how Tennyson uses the meter, along with poetic devices, to reflect the action in the poem.

The first stanza opens with a repetition of the phrase "half a league." It sets up a cadence like the soldiers riding on their horses. The beginning "h" sound and repeating the phrase three times creates the impression that the men and animals are barely trudging along. Line 3 is likely an allusion to the famous line in Psalm 23 that states, "Yea, though I walk through the valley of the shadow of death . . . " This foreshadows the outcome of the battle.

Line 4 identifies the number of soldiers that rode into battle. Tennyson does not give a lot of detail right away, assuming that people of the time would have been aware of the details of current events. In line 5, the cadence picks up as the men receive the command to go forward and charge for the guns. In the first few lines, they seem to be trudging toward "the valley of Death." Now they begin to charge into it. Lines 7 and 8 repeat lines 3 and 4 almost verbatim, further emphasizing the change in cadence.

The second stanza begins by repeating line 5, "Forward, the Light Brigade!" The speaker repeats the command and does a quick jump into the mind of the soldiers asking, "Was there a man dismay'd?" The brief switch brings out the human aspect of the battle. The orders had been messed up, but the soldiers didn't know they were given in error. Lines 13 to 15 reveal their character. Soldiers are trained not to question their orders. They did as they were trained to do and rode into the battle, even though it was obvious that this was going to be a suicide mission. The last two lines of this stanza repeat the last two lines of the first. This type of repetition is called a refrain and serves to emphasize the action.

Next comes the description of the brave charge into battle. Repetition occurs again in lines 18 to 20. Repeating a word or phrase at the beginning of a line is a poetic device called anaphora. Sound again plays a part in this group of lines. The hard /k/ sound at the beginning of the line gives way to softer sounds in the second stressed syllable. You can almost hear the sounds of the cannon being fired, then echoing through the valley as the soldiers charge through on their horses.

Lines 21 and 22 further develop this feeling. The picture shows they are charging into this valley, being shot at from all sides, yet "Boldly they rode and well." This time, instead of going into "the valley of Death," they are going "into the jaws of Death,/Into the mouth of hell." By giving death physical features, Tennyson employs the poetic device of personification. This serves to bring death into the scene as an active participant, not just the result of a battle. The last two lines of the stanza echo the refrain of the previous stanza but don't repeat them exactly.

The fourth stanza describes the battle. The challenge the soldiers of the Light Brigade faced is made even clearer. They wield only sabers while the Cossacks and Russians are heavily armed with guns and cannons. Notice the sounds of the words Tennyson used. The /f/ and /s/ sounds are reminiscent of the sound of sabers slashing through the air. The harsher sounds like /g/ and /ch/ are intermixed, giving the feeling that at least some of the sabers have made contact with their targets. Indeed, this is verified in lines 33, 35, and 36.

Early Genius

It is well known that Wolfgang Amadeus Mozart showed early genius at age five when he composed what we know as "Twinkle, Twinkle, Little Star" or the "Alphabet Song." Tennyson, too, showed early genius. He wrote a six-thousand-line epic poem when he was only twelve years old. He published a book of poems in 1827 when he was eighteen, and in 1830 and 1832. These last two volumes were harshly criticized as was the custom of critics at the time. But he took it personally and did not publish again for nine years. By 1850, he was one of Britain's most popular poets. He went on to write *Idylls of the King* and became Poet Laureate. He died at age eighty-three and is buried in Poet's Corner at Westminster Abbey in London.

Alfred, Lord Tennyson

The intensity of the battle is further developed through the verbs used at the beginning of most lines in this stanza: "Flash'd," "Sabring," "Charging," "Plunged," "Reel'd," and "Shatter'd." The brigade is relentless. In line 33, they break through the line. By line 36, the enemy is "Shatter'd and sunder'd." *Sunder* means "to break apart or sever," so they did as they were ordered. The refrain states that they then retreated, but there were no longer six hundred.

In the middle of this stanza is an interesting line. It is another one of those quick switches to a different perspective than that of the speaker. In this case, "All the world wonder'd" about the courageous charge against the well-fortified enemy. Overall, the poem is purposely focused on the scene at hand. This going in and out of the action jars the senses. It shifts the focus from the brutality of war to the human side of war. It also highlights the soldiers' character, building the case for the command in the last stanza.

Now the battle is over, but they have to return the same way they came. The first five lines of stanza 5 are the same as those in stanza 3 when they entered the valley, with one exception: one set of cannon is now behind them instead of in front of them. Lines 44 and 45 state the inevitable outcome: "While horse and hero fell,/They that had fought so well." Again, there is this shift from looking at the battle to looking at the individuals. Their courage is evident as they go through part three of the suicidal attack. Line 48 implies that "All that was left of them" was not very many.

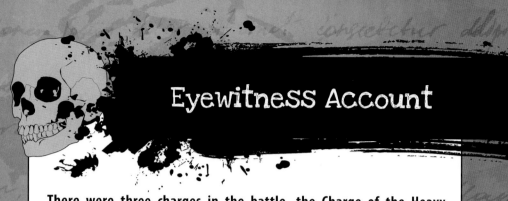

Eyewitness Account

There were three charges in the battle, the Charge of the Heavy Brigade, the Thin Red Line, and the Charge of the Light Brigade. Here is an eyewitness account by General Lord George Paget of the soldiers returning from the final one, the Charge of the Light Brigade:

> *On our return from the charge, the Light Brigade collected, as it were, on the slope of the hill looking towards Balaclava and remained there, some hours, on the chance of their services being again required. For some time stragglers and loose horses kept hobbling home, each being received by a hearty cheer at his unexpected appearance. There was then counting up of losses. A roll was soon called, and a melancholy ceremony it was, each narrating where they last saw a missing comrade, and all bewailing the known loss of many an old friend. It was a sad list indeed!*[2]

The final stanza has only six lines. The battle is over, and the speaker inserts himself into the scene to make a plea to the reader. He has been building up to this with the quick switches to another perspective. He has tugged at heartstrings throughout the story, showing the men's courage and character. He believes they should be remembered. "When can their glory fade?/O the wild charge they made!" One last quick switch to "All the world wondered" again, reinforcing the human element, the wonder of what kind of man would perform that kind of deed, knowing it was not wise. He finished with the command to honor them, again using anaphora for emphasis.

Remember, the Poet Laureate of England wrote this poem. Part of his purpose was to edify the masses with poetry. With this work, Tennyson shined a light on what was good and noble in the hearts of Englishmen. The poem itself, since it is still being read today, answered that call to honor those men.

Further Study Questions

1. Trace the progress of the battle stanza by stanza. Use this as a reference when answering the next few questions. Find all the instances of repetition in the poem. How does this affect the cadence for that particular section of the narrative?

2. Each stanza has a different number of lines, making it impossible to have a consistent rhyme scheme. Yet Tennyson seems to have some kind of rhyme pattern in mind. Go through the poem and note the rhyme scheme for each stanza. Do you see any pattern or reason for his choice of rhyming words? (When a word ends in "ed," pronounce it as /ed/ to keep the meter and produce a true rhyme with "hundred.")

3. Notice that Tennyson did not publish the name of the "someone" who had blundered. Read this account of the "someone" who gave the order: http://en.wikipedia.org/wiki/Louis_Nolan. List several reasons why Tennyson might not have wanted to go so far as to name the person.

4. Read other poems written from the perspective of the victors such as Henry van Dyke's "America's Welcome Home," Henry Wadsworth Longfellow's "The Cumberland," or Frances Miles Finch's "The Blue and The Gray." How are the soldiers in those poems portrayed? Does victory or defeat make a difference?

5. It has been said that our view of history is skewed because "the winner gets to write history." This poem is written from the point of view of the losers. What do you think the Russian soldiers thought when they saw the British coming at them with sabers? Write a poem as if you are the Poet Laureate for the tsar of Russia and include the impressions of the Cossack and Russian soldiers.

"Vigil Strange I Kept on the Field One Night"
Walt Whitman
(1819–1892)

There is nothing so noble as death on a smoky battlefield, dying for a cause you believe in. In normal times, when a hero dies, he is lifted up before the eyes of the world to be honored and admired. During the Civil War, many soldiers died as heroes, but they were simply buried on the battlefield, without being honored, and often without even being known by name.

Whitman's Background

As a nurse during the Civil War, Walt Whitman was familiar with dying soldiers and their need to be appreciated. He wrote a selection of poems published as *Drum-Taps* about the Civil War and what he experienced. Critic Huck Gutman contends "for the poet the dominating metaphor for the war is a hospital, filled with injured men who must be nursed or, if dying, comforted."[1]

In this poem, Whitman imagines that same type of care and nurturing on the battlefield. *Drum-Taps* was later rolled into his larger work titled *Leaves of Grass*. *Drum-Taps* focused on the consequences of the war, not the war itself. Whitman did not choose sides in the war. He spent his energy ministering to the wounded, something he started in the winter of

Walt Whitman

1862 when he set out looking for his brother George after the Battle of Fredericksburg in Virginia.

When he arrived, he looked for his brother among the wounded. He was so moved by what he saw in the field hospital that he spent the rest of the war volunteering as a comforter, sometimes being called upon to act as nurse as well. He eventually had a breakdown and had to retreat to his home in Brooklyn to recover.

Leaves of Grass

Walt Whitman published only one title, *Leaves of Grass*, but he periodically added poems to the book and republished it under the same name. The first edition included twelve poems but was not well received due to its socially unacceptable topic of the body and what some in polite society considered coarse language. Before the war, the twelve-poem edition of *Leaves of Grass* was so controversial that when he wanted to publish his poems about the Civil War, he could not find a publisher, nor was he welcome in Washington, D.C., where he served as nurse for the wounded. Whitman scholar Martin G. Murray explains: "Scorn by 'Society' prevented Whitman from securing a good government berth to support himself and his wartime hospital ministry. Even a recommendation from Ralph Waldo Emerson elicited a chilly response from Secretary of the Treasury Salmon Chase, who dismissed the poet's *Leaves* as a 'very bad book,' and the poet himself as 'a decidedly disreputable person.'"[2]

When President Lincoln was assassinated, Whitman wrote two poems that captured the public's mood, "O Captain! My Captain!" and "When Lilacs Last in the Door-yard Bloomed." It was not until he achieved popular success that a publisher was willing to take a chance on his war poems, *Drum-Taps*. *Drum-Taps* and these poems about Lincoln were incorporated into *Leaves of Grass* for its fourth edition in 1867. The final publication of *Leaves of Grass* included almost four hundred poems. Although his books were controversial and not a financial success during his life, he was recognized as a new and important voice in American literature.

Vigil Strange I Kept on the Field One Night

VIGIL strange I kept on the field one night;

When you my son and my comrade dropt at my side that day,

One look I but gave which your dear eyes return'd with a look I
   shall never forget;

One touch of your hand to mine O boy, reach'd up as you lay on
   the ground,

Then onward I sped in the battle; the even-contested battle,

Till late in the night reliev'd to the place at last again I made my
   way;

Found you in death so cold dear comrade, found your body son
   of responding kisses, (never again on earth responding);

Bared your face in the starlight—curious the scene—cool blew
   the moderate night-wind,

Long there and then in vigil I stood, dimly around me the battlefield spreading;

Vigil wondrous and vigil sweet there in the fragrant silent night,

But not a tear fell, not even a long-drawn sigh—Long, long I
   gazed,

Then on the earth partially reclining sat by your side leaning my
   chin in my hands;

Passing sweet hours, immortal and mystic hours with you
   dearest comrade—not a tear, not a word,

Vigil of silence, love and death, vigil for you my son and my
   soldier,

As onward silently stars aloft, eastward new ones upward stole;

Vigil final for you brave boy, (I could not save you, swift was
   your death,

I faithfully loved you and cared for you living—I think we shall
  surely meet again,)
Till at latest lingering of the night, indeed just as the dawn
  appear'd,
My comrade I wrapt in his blanket, envelop'd well his form,
Folded the blanket well, tucking it carefully over head and
  carefully under feet;
And there and then and bathed by the rising sun, my son in his
  grave, in his rude-dug grave I deposited,
Ending my vigil strange with that—vigil of night and battle-field
  dim,
Vigil for boy of responding kisses, (never again on earth
  responding—)
Vigil for comrade swiftly slain, vigil I never forget, how as day
  brighten'd,
I rose from the chill ground and folded my soldier well in his
  blanket,
And buried him where he fell.

Whitman's Lament

The Civil War is not referenced directly in the poem, so the setting, an unnamed battlefield, is derived from the historical facts of the poet's life. This poem is Whitman's way of giving honor to those many unnamed soldiers who died in the war and were buried on the battlefield without so much as a grave marker. It is written in free verse, a poetic form that does not follow a specific meter or rhyme. The lines are different lengths, and they follow the thoughts of the speaker and the natural rhythms of speech. The analysis that follows reads as a series of vignettes, viewed through the speaker's eyes as his focus shifts around the scene.

Lines 1–5

The first line introduces the topic, calling it a "Vigil strange." In the poem, Whitman reverses the normal order of words to create emphasis and draw the reader's attention. In line 2, he identifies the reason for the poem: the speaker's friend has been wounded in the battle and is lying on the battlefield. In line 3, they make eye contact and exchange "a look I shall never forget." Whitman uses ambiguity here, not telling us exactly what kind of look it was. It could have been a look of horror, fear, resignation, returned love, or peace. There is no indication here, and we never find out.

In line 4, that look extends to a touch. Whitman again reverses the order of things. The touch comes before the hand reaches out, jarring the reader a little, forcing him to see the hand reaching out to make that touch. The look, the touch, and then in line 5, he goes back to his duty and the battle. Notice specifically that the speaker calls it "the even-contested battle." Whitman did not take sides in the war, so this is a reflection of his stance.

Lines 6–11: Arrival and Start of the Vigil

Night falls. The battle stops for the night, and the speaker returns to where his friend fell. He "in death so cold dear comrade, found your body." Up to this point, Whitman has mentioned individual body parts—eyes and hands—making them come alive by relating them to different sensory images. He does so again in line 7 with "son of responding kisses, (never again on earth responding)." But in between, he contrasts what was in life to what is in death by referring to the boy as a "body." This is similar to the kind of distance a doctor would have between himself and a person by referring to him as a case instead of a patient.

Line 8 has a lot going on. The boy's face is "bared in the starlight." Whitman zeroes in on a body part again, the face, and provides the detail about starlight that illuminates him. He then takes a step back and observes how "curious the scene." Here is another of Whitman's reverse word order reminiscent of the character Yoda in *Star Wars*.

After taking a step back, he adds another sensation, "cool blew the moderate night-wind." "Moderate" echoes the thought earlier about the even-contested battle. Line 9 has the speaker standing over the body in a vigil with "dimly around me the battlefield spreading." If this were a movie scene, you would have the camera zooming out to take in the carnage all around him while he stands vigil for this one person.

Line 10 seems to echo the words of the Christmas song "Silent Night" with "Vigil wondrous and vigil sweet" in the "fragrant silent night." Even with the battlefield of dead soldiers all around, there is a sense of peace between these two. The silence carries over to the man who is standing vigil, as "not a tear fell, not even a long-drawn sigh." He simply "gazed" with a profound stillness.

Lines 12–17: A Slight Shift in Position

At some point, the speaker shifts his position and sits next to the body, partially reclining while "Passing sweet hours, immortal and mystic" with the boy. He has now passed into a kind of otherworldly existence in the starlight and silence. In line 13, he refers to the boy as "dearest comrade," and in line 14 as "my son and my soldier." It is almost like he is thinking back through the different facets of their relationship, this "Vigil of silence, love and death."

Line 15 contains the second reference to stars. The first, in line 8, has starlight illuminating the boy's face, but here the stars show the passage of time. There is the sense of being one with the universe, which falls in line with Whitman's beliefs about an afterlife that shows up in lines 16 and 17. The soldier continues to reminisce, ending with "I think we shall surely meet again."

Lines 18–21: The Burial

In line 18, dawn arrives. The nighttime vigil is over. The boy is back to being "my comrade" on the battlefield, and the speaker wraps his "form" in his blanket for burial. He goes on to describe the loving ritual he performed as he wrapped the body. In line 21, the form is bathed in sunlight, whereas before his face was bared by the starlight. The grave is "rude-dug," meaning shallow so the body would be close to the surface.

Lines 22–26: Honor Through Remembering

The last five lines of the poem sum up the events that took place. The speaker uses the word *vigil* three times in lines 23 and 24. It is almost as if he is honoring the boy one last time, both as friend, "Vigil for boy of responding kisses," and soldier, "Vigil for comrade swiftly slain." The vigil was one he would never forget, just as he would never forget the look in the boy's eyes the day before. The final scene has him rising "from the chill ground," wrapping the soldier in his blanket, and then burying him "where he fell." Then it would be time to get back to the war.

Poetic Devices

This poem is written in free verse. It has no specific rhyme or meter, but it does have constraints, mostly imposed by the poet on himself. For example, notice how the first and last lines are short compared to the rest of the lines. Those two lines sum up the whole poem. You could skip everything else and still understand what took place on a surface level. However, it is all the description and the nuance in between that tells the real story.

Whitman's poetry is rich in sensory experience. He gives details that give the reader a sense of what the speaker is going through. In the nighttime scene especially, his choice of words causes the reader to experience every nuance of sound, sight, and touch.

Whitman liked to work with ambiguity, and this poem is a great example. Throughout the poem, the reader is never certain of the relationship between the older soldier and the young one. It could be a father and a son, or two lovers, or two human beings cosmically connected. Ambiguity shows up again twice in line 21. First, when the wrapped body is "bathed by the rising sun," it should be read literally, but "bathed" could also be interpreted as cleansed or renewed. Later in that line, there is a reference to the body being "deposited" in a shallow grave. Again, beyond the literal meaning, it could also mean an investment, as in the speaker had invested in the boy's life, and hoped to reap something from it in the afterlife.

Bridging Two Worlds

Until his brother George was wounded, Whitman stayed out of the war. But as he visited the field hospitals in search of his brother, the wounded soldiers aroused his compassion. He volunteered to work with the wounded, leading to surprise developments in his writing. Angel Price writes of Whitman's experience:

> *Whitman's practice of writing letters home for soldiers began during those first days spent in camp with George at Falmouth. Many of the soldiers were illiterate or simply inarticulate, and as a man of letters Whitman found great joy and responsibility in writing for his wounded men. Upon leaving the protected atmosphere of Brooklyn and arriving in the world of soldiers, Whitman realized the chasm that separated the soldier's existence and that of the civilian's world. Whitman's writing—verse, letters, newspaper articles and notebooks—created a link between these two worlds and a better understanding of the unique suffering on each side.*

In some ways, Whitman's role as psychological nurse to the wounded extends to a surrogate and psychological bridge between two distinct worlds during the Civil War.[3]

One of Whitman's poems in the original *Leaves of Grass* was titled "Song of Myself," in which Whitman portrays himself as a symbol of the common man. He was trying to fulfill Emerson's vision for poets who speak for America with a unique voice. Though he started out by producing poetry with great shock value, it seems the war changed his perspective and molded him, truly giving him the voice of the common man. In the end, his song was no longer about himself.

Further Study Questions

1. As the name implies, "free verse" has no limitations on its form. However, poets who use it say it requires some kind of structure for the poem to be any good. See if you can identify any structural elements and poetic devices in this poem. Look for things such as use of punctuation, alliteration, repetition, internal rhymes, choice of words, and associations within the poem.

2. What does *night* signify in this poem?

3. Why do you think Whitman put some of the speaker's thoughts in parentheses?

4. Study Whitman's use of the five senses in describing his scenes. How does it draw you into the poem?

5. Write your own war poem in free verse. If you need ideas, you can take this poem and rewrite it where the characters are father and son, or maybe brothers on opposite sides of the war, Union and Confederacy. Another possibility is to write about an incident in a news story you have seen or heard. Use some of the literary devices you found in question 1 to help you.

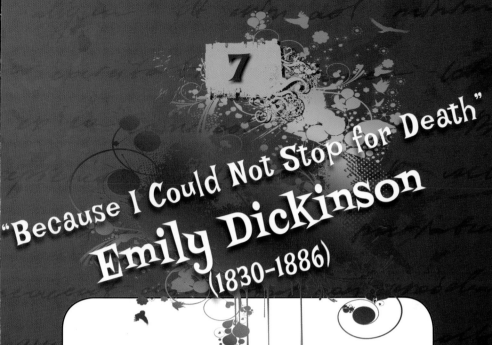

"Because I Could Not Stop for Death"
Emily Dickinson
(1830–1886)

Everyone has a date with death, so Emily Dickinson decided to make it literal, using the real-life experience of courtship. Death is a suitor who takes the speaker on a carriage ride. In the guise of a suitor, death is portrayed as something interesting, even desirable. Critic Eleanor Wilner explains, "In her fear of death, she constantly invoked it, recreated it, rehearsed it, even reveled in it."[1] Welcome to the world of Emily Dickinson.

Unconventional Beginning

Many of Dickinson's 1,789 poems included themes of death and physical and mental suffering. It is difficult to tell how many of these were autobiographical. Dickinson requested that her sister destroy all her personal correspondence upon her death, which she apparently did, so there's no way to compare her inner thoughts to her poetry.

Most of what we know of Dickinson's life is gleaned from letters, notes, and correspondence collected from friends. Dickinson was a recluse and lived in the family home in Amherst, Massachusetts, her entire life, never traveling far. She had a brother and a sister. She lived with her sister; neither of them married. Next door, their married brother, Austin, lived with his wife, Mabel Todd Loomis. Outside of this family circle, Dickinson saw fewer and fewer people as she grew older, possibly because of a physical ailment or mental breakdowns.

When Dickinson was thirty-two years old, she read an article in the *Atlantic Monthly* with advice to budding writers. She sent a letter to the author, Thomas Wentworth Higginson, along with four of her poems asking for his opinion of them. Though he thought the poems odd, he inquired about her background and asked her to send more poems.

They became correspondents, with Higginson acting as a sort of mentor and advisor. Although he praised her poems, he didn't think the world was ready for her unconventional style and form. He advised against publication. This was no problem for Dickinson as she was a private person. Only four of her poems were published during her lifetime.

Differences Between Dickinson and Brontë

Although Emily Brontë's and Dickinson's lives shared many similarities (see sidebar in the Brontë chapter), their views of death were different. In "No Coward Soul Is Mine," Brontë indicates no fear of death. Her steadfast faith in God and belief in an eternity free from the pains of earth led her to treat death as a natural passage from one life to the next. Dickinson, on the other hand, wrestled with the idea of death. Many of her poems include images of themes related to death. "Because I Could Not Stop for Death" is unusual for her in that death is quite benevolent. In most of her poetry, her vision of death includes obliteration, such as "I Felt a Funeral in My Brain" (Poem 280) or "I Heard a Fly Buzz" (Poem 465).

Higginson and her sister-in-law published the rest after her death. Because none had titles, they were given numbers. Over the years, different editors used different numbers. This poem is typically known as either Poem 479 or Poem 712, depending on the editor's system used.

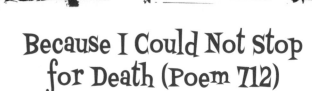

Because I Could Not Stop for Death (Poem 712)

Because I could not stop for Death—
He kindly stopped for me—
The Carriage held but just Ourselves—
And Immortality.

We slowly drove—He knew no haste
And I had put away
My labor and my leisure too,
For His Civility—

We passed the School, where Children strove
At Recess—in the Ring—
We passed the Fields of Gazing Grain—
We passed the Setting Sun—

Or rather—He passed us—
The Dews drew quivering and chill—
For only Gossamer, my Gown—
My Tippet—only Tulle—

We paused before a House that seemed
A Swelling of the Ground—
The Roof was scarcely visible—
The Cornice—in the Ground—

Since then—'tis Centuries—and yet
Feels shorter than the Day
I first surmised the Horses' Heads
Were toward Eternity—

A Date With Death

Have you ever lost anyone close to you? How did it affect you? Death is the end of every man and woman, yet most people fear it. In "Because I Could Not Stop for Death," Dickinson turns that view around. She presents death as a date, using the courtship rituals of her day. Although it is a little creepy to think of going on a date with death, the overall effect in this case is one of peace and calm. Critic Allen Tate points out that Dickinson was a master at creating "a tension between abstraction and sensation in which the two elements may be, of course, distinguished logically, but not really." That tension is evident throughout this poem. The abstraction is Death as a suitor; the sensation is the strong emotional element normally present in a courtship.

The first two lines of the poem catapult us into the storyline. The speaker's seemingly full life is abruptly halted when Death appears. There is the sense that the woman is unprepared for death, and this will come out again later in the poem. From this point forward, the pace slows and the courtship begins. The carriage stops and picks her up, then proceeds on a journey. But Death and the woman are not alone. They have a chaperone named Immortality. Obviously, this relationship is permanent.

In the second stanza, the relationship develops. Look at the pronouns. At this point, they are still separate. The speaker uses "I" when talking about laying aside her work

Emily Dickinson

and her amusements for this ride. "He knew no haste" and "His Civility" are observations about her suitor. These references to her suitor also speak to the ritual of courtship. Dickinson's contemporaries would have recognized these references. Even though the details may be lost in modern times, the imagery still holds the essence of her intent.

Dickinson is able to convey a lot of meaning by referencing whole bodies of thought in just a few words. For example, the third stanza is a poetic representation of "my life flashed before my eyes." It begins with children and ends with the setting sun. The children represent youth; the setting sun represents the end of life. So, in twenty-four words, Dickinson covers a life span and still keeps within the gentle pace of the carriage ride. This poem is a great example of how a poet's ability to capture thoughts in just a few words makes poetry both rewarding and a lot of work at the same time.

In stanza 3, notice how often the speaker uses "we." There is an intimacy that did not exist before. The transition from stanza 3 to stanza 4 seems to describe the actual point of death. Stanza 3 ends with "We passed the Setting Sun—" and stanza 4 continues with "Or rather—He passed us—." In addition to the idea of the setting sun as the end of life, there is the switch from light into darkness. This is not stated specifically but mentions of dews and chill come with nightfall.

Stanza 4 mentions the woman's clothing. Gossamer is a thin fabric, not appropriate for the cold. Her tippet, a shoulder wrap of sorts, was made of tulle, a lightweight netting that would not hold in bodily warmth. These articles of clothing are not appropriate for the nighttime, another indication that the speaker was not ready for death when it came.

The fifth stanza describes a house, albeit an odd one. The house is a "Swelling of the Ground" and "The Roof was scarcely visible." The cornice, an ornamental molding on the roof, is in the ground. This underground house is her burial spot, her grave. She has come home.

Just like movies, poetry can also have surprise endings. This poem does not disappoint. Stanza 6 drops the bomb. Poem 712 is not happening in real time. It is the memory of the speaker's death hundreds of years in the past but remembered like it was yesterday.

Dickinson's Grammar Style

The most obvious feature of Dickinson's poetry is its unique punctuation and capitalization. It is noticeable even before reading the poem. She used this style in all her poems. Although she never explains why she writes this way, there seems to be a consistency to her use of these elements.

The capitalized words are almost exclusively nouns. This could be to emphasize the noun, or simply to make the reader think about the word instead of quickly reading past it to get to the next word. Sometimes she includes the adjectives that modify the noun, as in "Setting Sun" and "Horse's Heads." The dashes have the same effect, especially when used at the end of a line. They make the reader pause. Sometimes this is for dramatic effect, such as lines 10 to 16, where each of the seven lines ends with a dash. When used within a line, the dashes connect thoughts, adding detail to the image she is trying to convey.

Metaphorically Speaking

The courtship ritual serves as an extended metaphor that goes throughout the poem. The ritual includes the initial meeting; a chaperone in the form of Immortality; a long, slow drive; and an end to the trip that's not really an end but only the beginning of Eternity. Dickinson uses personification within her metaphor. Death is personified as a suitor. The poem never identifies Death as a suitor directly, but the imagery of courtship throughout implies this idea. Another instance of personification occurs in line 13 when the sun is referred to as "He." At first, in line 12, the sun is just the sun, as in "We passed the Setting Sun—", but in the next line the characterization changes when Dickinson uses "He" to reference the sun.

Using Meter and Language to Convey Meaning

Keeping in line with the extended metaphor of a carriage ride, Dickinson uses meter and language to imply the movement of the carriage. The meter is one commonly used in hymns, which would have been part of her Puritan upbringing. This poem, like many of her poems, can be sung to tunes such as "Amazing Grace" or even "The Yellow Rose of Texas." Even though the music is different, the beats of music fit the meter of the words.

To see why this works, let's take a deeper look at what is going on. First, there is the overall rhythm. Recall that rhythm is determined by the number of feet in a line and that feet are determined by the stressed syllables in a line. A foot consists of one stressed syllable in combination with one or more unstressed syllables, and feet have names based on how the stressed and unstressed syllables are combined.

This poem alternates using iambic tetrameter and iambic trimeter. Remember that the type of foot called an iamb consists of an unstressed syllable followed by a stressed syllable. In line 1, the stressed syllables are *cause, could, stop,* and *Death.* There are four beats, so the meter is labeled tetrameter, *tetra* meaning "four." In line 2, there are only three iambs, making it trimeter.

Poets often fudge the syllables a little and mix up the types of feet they use to fit in a few extra words. Dickinson does not do that here. Every foot in the poem is a perfect iamb; it has an unstressed syllable followed by a stressed syllable. There is one exception in this poem, and this is on purpose for dramatic effect. This switch occurs at the point of death, at the beginning of stanza 4. Because the meter has been so perfect up to this point, the meter change jolts the reader—a big clue that the poet is trying to convey something special at that point.

In this poem, meter serves another purpose. It echoes the cadence of the horses pulling the carriage. This is subtle, but it adds to the overall feeling of the poem. This poem also uses a poetic device called anaphora, which uses repetition. Anaphora is used to pull the poem together or emphasize a particular idea. In the third stanza, Dickinson uses "We passed" three times to emphasize the passage of time. As mentioned earlier, it is as if the speaker's life is passing before her eyes. Then Dickinson uses it again in the fourth stanza but changes it to "He passed," referring to the sun. Again, this is a subtle change, but it is these small things that add up to great poetry.

Rhyme, or Its Absence

Rhyme goes hand in hand with rhythm. We are accustomed to hearing rhyme, first in nursery rhymes, then in popular music. Rhyme makes it easier to remember a song and makes it flow. Dickinson uses rhyme in an interesting way here. For the most part, the lines do not truly rhyme, but they are close to rhyming. This is called slant rhyme, half rhyme, or false rhyme. Examples of this are "away" and "Civility" in stanza 2, "chill" and "Tulle" in stanza 4, and "Day" and "Eternity" in stanza 6. Stanza 3 does not rhyme at all, while stanza 5 repeats the same word. The only stanza with true rhyme is the first one, where "me" and "Immortality" rhyme. By doing this, she calls attention to one word: Immortality.

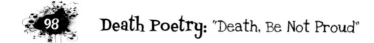

You could say that is the theme of the poem, or maybe even a question Dickinson has about the afterlife.

Imagery

Dickinson's poems tend to be concise and convey deep meaning. She achieves this effect by employing a variety of poetic devices. Some of those previously mentioned are rhyme, rhythm and meter, and metaphors, both regular and extended. Imagery—the pictures the words bring to mind—plays a big part in this poem, too. Many of the images are emphasized through alliteration. This repetition of the sounds at the beginning of words joins them together and intensifies their meaning. Examples abound in this poem, such as "labor" and "leisure," "Recess" and "Ring," and "Tippet" and "Tulle." The words and the images they convey are linked together.

The whole poem presents a unified image, tied together by the poetic devices. First, there is the extended metaphor of a carriage ride, providing the action in the poem. Then there is the cadence of the words that echo the carriage ride, adding sound to the action. And last, there is the image of the horses' heads turned toward eternity. The final image is of the horses' head jutting forward, and the last word in the poem is "Eternity." The horses leave us on an endless journey, which closes the circle started in stanza 1 with "Immortality."

Was the World Ready?

Higginson did not think the world was ready for Dickinson's poetry, even after her death. He states, "The impression of a wholly new and original poetic genius was as distinct on my mind at the first reading of these four poems as it is now, after thirty years of further knowledge; and with it came the problem never yet solved, what place ought to be assigned in literature to what is so remarkable, yet so elusive of criticism."[2]

Before publishing her poems, he edited her punctuation, diction, and rhyme to make it more palatable to the public. Since then, Dickinson's poems have been published in their original form. Interestingly, it is this form, along with its style and depth, which gives her poetry its unique place in literature.

Further Study Questions

1. Some poems tell a story and can be structured like a movie. A movie starts with an inciting incident, goes through action scenes and reaches a climax, then concludes by tying up any loose ends in the story line. Does this poem fit into that sequence? If so, relate each stanza to part of a story sequence. What elements of suspense does Dickinson use to keep the reader reading?

2. This poem relies heavily on imagery of time passing. Which words or phrases give the feeling of time and its passing?

3. There are two stopping points along the journey mentioned in the poem. What are they and what do they signify?

4. Originally, this poem was published without the dashes and mid-line capitalization. Rewrite the poem without those elements, adding punctuation wherever you think it is needed. Does it change the poem at all? Is the poem improved by removing the unconventional style? Which version do you like better?

5. It is said that iambic meter is the most common pattern of English speech. Listen to other people's speech to see if this is true. Take note of five instances where you hear iambic meter in someone's conversation or the teacher's lecture.

8

"To an Athlete Dying Young"
A. E. Housman
(1859–1936)

Is there ever a good time to die? You may have heard something along the lines of, "If you have to die, you may as well go out in a blaze of glory." That is the idea behind this poem, but is it a valid point? After studying the poem, you will have a chance to explore the validity through some of the questions at the end.

The Great Classical Scholar

Alfred Edward Housman, better known as A. E. Housman, has been deemed one of the greatest classical scholars of all time. He was born in Fockbury, Worcestershire, England, and although he attended St. John's College,

Oxford, on an academic scholarship, he did not graduate. No one is certain why, but it had a profound effect on his professional life. He would forever try to prove his scholarship through his work rather than a degree. It eventually paid off. After seeing the quality of his published critical analyses of ancient scholars, he was offered a Professorship of Latin at University College London. Later, he would become a professor of Latin at Trinity College, Cambridge. His editions of the Roman poets Juvenal, Manilius, and Lucan are still viewed as the authoritative texts.

Outside of his job, he was a recluse. He kept to himself, never married, and had no known companions. He was strange and forlorn, and his poetry reflects that. His works fit into a category labeled Romantic pessimism, a type of Romanticism where one's own suffering is projected onto the world as a universal truth. One critic notes that Housman "was a pessimist interested only in the tragic aspects of life. Everywhere he looked, he saw cause for disillusionment and a sense of the vanity of men's efforts."[1]

Although he was first and foremost a classical scholar, most students know him for his poetry. His first book of poems, *A Shropshire Lad*, was published in 1896. Whereas his professional work was all about precision and correcting errors made by scholars and scribes in the past, his poetry revealed an emotional side, perhaps because he had no relational outlet for it.

To an Athlete Dying Young

The time you won your town the race
We chaired you through the market-place;
Man and boy stood cheering by,
And home we brought you shoulder-high.

To-day, the road all runners come,
Shoulder-high we bring you home,
And set you at your threshold down,
Townsman of a stiller town.

Smart lad, to slip betimes away
From fields where glory does not stay,
And early though the laurel grows
It withers quicker than the rose.

Eyes the shady night has shut
Cannot see the record cut,
And silence sounds no worse than cheers
After earth has stopped the ears:

Now you will not swell the rout
Of lads that wore their honours out,
Runners whom renown outran
And the name died before the man.

So set, before its echoes fade,
The fleet foot on the sill of shade,
And hold to the low lintel up
The still-defended challenge-cup.

And round that early-laurelled head
Will flock to gaze the strengthless dead,
And find unwithered on its curls
The garland briefer than a girl's.

An Elegy

The title of the poem clues the reader in to several things: it is an elegy, a poem of lament for the dead; the subject is an athlete; and the athlete is young. Knowing these details sets the reader's expectation and helps with understanding the poem from the first line. Even with that much laid out up front, there are still a lot of discoveries to be made.

The poem is set up in seven stanzas of four lines each. The rhyme scheme is *aabb*. The rhyming lines often form one thought and make interpretation easier. Each line is written in tetrameter, meaning there are four beats, or feet, to each line. Most of the lines are iambic tetrameter, but there are some instances of troachic tetrameter with catalexis. Iambic describes a foot with two beats, the first unstressed, the second stressed. Trochaic is the opposite, a foot with two beats, the first one stressed, the second unstressed. When Housman uses troachic tetrameter, he usually drops a syllable from the last foot, known as catalexis. The second stanza has two examples of each:

To-**day**, the **road** all **run**ners **come**,	*iambic tetrameter*
Shoulder-**high** we **bring** you **home**,	*trochaic tetrameter with catalexis*
And **set** you **at** your **thres**hold **down**,	*iambic tetrameter*
Townsman **of** a **still**er **town**.	*trochaic tetrameter with catalexis*

The meter makes this poem an easy read, and the surface meaning is easy to understand. But there are occasional glimpses of undercurrents, giving the reader the sense there is a lot more to it. These undercurrents will be explored in the next section.

Glory Days

The first stanza shows a snapshot of a hometown hero. The poem reflects the customs in hundreds of small towns throughout England in the 1800s. The hero has won a race as a representative of the town. The wording used, "you won your town the race," is awkward, but it explains why the townspeople are so excited about this young man. They "chaired him through the market-place," meaning they hoisted him up in the air like you see happening today after the final play of a game in sports.

In lines 3 and 4, the crowd is cheering as "home we brought you shoulder-high." Again, the townspeople show the athlete honor by lifting him up as they move through the town.

Lines 5 and 6 offer an abrupt change in tone and story. The time has changed to "To-day," and the race is one "all runners" run, the road that leads to death. The speaker notes that they are bringing the athlete home "Shoulder-high" again. But this time he is set down, not continually

A. E. Housman

lifted and cheered as in the first stanza. The townsmen in his new home are "of a stiller town"—a cemetery. The contrast between the two trips carrying the athlete shoulder high is an example of poetic irony. First, he is lifted shoulder high by friends to honor his victory; then his casket is lifted onto their shoulders to honor his passing.

The next stanza serves as the speaker's commentary on the fleetingness of glory. This is the first insight into the speaker's mind. He calls the lad smart for slipping away from "fields" where glory does not stay. These would be the playing fields common to many sports where heroes come and go. But since Housman was a classical scholar, he is likely using allusion to contrast this with the Elysian Fields of Greek mythology, the final resting place of the heroic and the virtuous. Lines 11 and 12 present this fleeting time frame using another reference to Greece. He references leaves of laurel, alluding to the crowns given to Olympic athletes, and compares them to the fast-withering rose.

In the next eight lines, the speaker enumerates the benefits of dying young while at the height of glory. He gives four benefits, one in each couplet. The first one, in lines 13 and 14, states that eyes closed in death will not see the record broken. Second, in lines 15 and 16, he will not experience the crowds cheering for another once he is dead. Lines 17 and 18 speak of a "rout," a rapid retreat after defeat, and "Of lads that wore their honours out." The young athlete will not be among those who stayed in their sport too long and left in defeat instead of in glory. The next couplet speaks of those whose fame faded over time, "And the name died before the man." That will never happen to him. He will be immortalized at his moment of glory.

The sixth stanza imagines the dead on the threshold mentioned in line 7. The "sill" and "lintel" are both parts of a doorway. The lintel is the beam across the top of a doorway. The speaker encourages him to go through the doorway quickly, before the echoes of the cheering crowds fade, and to hold up the "still-defended challenge-cup" as a reminder of his accomplishment. The challenge-cup was a trophy given to the current winner of an event. It would likely have the names of those who had won inscribed on a plate. He still had the cup so his death occurred before time for the next race came around.

Poems for a Lost Generation

Housman's book of poems, *A Shropshire Lad*, includes several poems about youth cut down in their prime, including "To an Athlete Dying Young." Critics have noted that "While *A Shropshire Lad* was slow to gain in popularity, the advent of war, first in the Boer War and then in World War I, gave the book widespread appeal due to its nostalgic depiction of brave English soldiers. Several composers created musical settings for Housman's work, deepening his popularity."[2]

The speaker peeks into the afterlife in the final stanza. In line 25, the "early-laurelled head" refers to the boy's youth, while the "strengthless dead" are all those who have died, some young, some old. In the afterlife, he still wears the laurel crown, but the crowd around him now is "strengthless," unable to lift him up in glory. They see the newly placed crown of laurel on his head, "unwithered," even though it is a "garland briefer than a girl's." In line 12, the speaker mentions how the crown withers quicker than a rose. Here, he points out it is "unwithered," even though it would normally fade faster than the flower garlands girls would put in their hair. His moment of glory would be preserved for eternity.

Poetic Devices

Housman sprinkles poetic devices throughout the poem. Some have already been mentioned, such as irony in the first two stanzas and the allusion to Greek classics in the third stanza. The third stanza also contains a simile in how the laurel "withers quicker than the rose." "Quicker than" is the comparison. Housman uses personification twice in the fourth stanza. In line 13, death "the shady night" shuts the eyes of the runner, and in line 16, the earth "has stopped the ears." He has given human attributes to the night and the earth. The fifth stanza contains an oxymoron, "silence sounds." Silence doesn't sound like anything; rather, it is the absence of sound. Stanza six has an example of synecdoche, a poetic device where a part is used to represent the whole. In this case, the "fleet foot" is used to represent the whole person getting ready to pass into the next life.

Two poetic devices are used throughout the poem. First, the whole poem is an apostrophe, an address to someone who is not there to respond. Second, Housman uses alliteration in almost every line.

Alliteration means the same sound appears in words in close proximity to one another. Two examples in the first line are "time" and "town," and "you" and "your." He also uses consonance, which is similar to alliteration, but the sounds are within the words instead of at the beginning.

Line 19 has both alliteration and consonance that work together. "Runners" and "renown" illustrate alliteration; "outran" repeats the "r" for consonance.

Echoes of Eternity

Housman uses sound imagery to develop his theme. He uses three words specifically to note different phases in the poem: "cheering" in line 3, "silence" in line 15, and "echoes" in line 21. "Cheering" occurs while the runner is alive and "silence" once he is dead. Then there are the "echoes" of the cheering crowds heard fading as he stands on the threshold between life and the afterlife. The speaker contends that the best time to die is while the echoes of achievement still reverberate in the hearts and minds of those left behind. According to the poem, this young man achieved that slice of immortality where the echoes will never fade away, implied by the word "unwithered" in line 27. In a sense, he found the eternal fountain of youth.

Further Study Questions

1. Death has many euphemisms, mild words or expressions used to refer to something unpleasant. Find all the different ways that Housman refers to death in this poem.

2. Print a copy of the poem and highlight all the instances of alliteration.

3. Although the speaker obviously celebrated along with the town, at times there seems to be envy under the surface. Do you think the speaker shows true appreciation and is honoring the athlete or is he envious of the young athlete? If you chose envy, what is he envious of—the glory the young man received or the fact that because he died young, that glory is preserved?

4. Do you think the speaker is young or old? Do you get the impression that maybe he was once carried into town in a field of glory and now his accomplishments have been forgotten? What in the poem are you basing your answers on?

5. Is dying young the only way to make glory last? Compare this list of famous people who died young [actors James Dean (24), Heath Ledger (28), and Marilyn Monroe (36); rapper Tupac Shakur (25); U.S. president John F. Kennedy (46); Princess Diana of Great Britain (36); and author Emily Brontë (30)] to this list of those who died after a long life [physicist Albert Einstein (76); missionary Mother Theresa of Calcutta (87); artists Michelangelo (89) and Pablo Picasso (91); and poet Alfred, Lord Tennyson (83)]. All of these people are renowned, but is there a difference in the type of renown or how they are remembered?

Sample Answers to Further Study Questions

Note: Questions that ask for reader opinions will vary. There is no one correct answer. Responses should, however, demonstrate a close reading of texts.

CHAPTER 1: "Death, Be Not Proud" John Donne (1572–1631)

1.

	1	Death, be not proud, though some have called thee	A
restatement	2	Mighty and dreadful, for thou art not so;	B
	3	For those whom thou think'st thou dost overthrow,	B
contrast	4	Die not, poor Death, nor yet canst thou kill me.	A

quatrain (bracketing lines 1–4)

2. Most of the answers are listed out in lines 9 to 14. The remaining answers will vary.

3. For example, line 4 has three instances of alliteration: "Die" and "Death," "not" and "nor," and "canst" and "kill." Find more in other lines.

4. Answers will vary.

5. Answers will vary, but the poems should be in the form of a sonnet as described in the chapter.

CHAPTER 2: "We Are Seven"
William Wordsworth (1770–1850)

1. Once the alliteration is identified, the answers will vary. The young girl tends to use alliteration more, giving her

speech a lilting, carefree sound. The adult sounds more reasoned and logical.

2. For example, in the second stanza, lines 6 and 7 have different feet in the same line. Line 13 starts with a trochaic foot if "Sisters" is pronounced normally, but it can be forced into an iambic foot by putting the accent on the second syllable instead of the first. In almost every instance of the word "seven," the type of foot changes.

3. The speaker is consistent in trying to use logic to persuade the young girl. It seems to have no effect on the little girl. In the end, the speaker realizes that all his reason will not change her mind.

4. Answers will vary.

5. Answers will vary.

CHAPTER 3: "No Coward Soul Is Mine"
Emily Brontë (1818–1848)

1. Words referring to the concept of light: Heaven's glories shine, faith shines, life, anchored, steadfast, immortality, love, animates, changes, sustains, creates, suns and universes, Being, Breath.

   Words referring to the concept of darkness: storm-troubled sphere, fear, worthless, withered, weeds, doubt, broods, Death, void, destroyed.

   Answers to this question will vary.

2. Answers will vary.

3. She means that although Death seems to be powerful, it cannot alter a single atom or its purpose.

4. Answers will vary.

5. Answers will vary.

CHAPTER 4: "Good-by" Ralph Waldo Emerson (1803–1882)

1. In this poem, Emerson seems to be breaking away from both the crowd (mentally) and the crowded city (physically). He acknowledges the great changes taking place in the first two stanzas but chooses to retreat in the last two stanzas.

2. Emerson emphasizes the worst aspects of a society: "Flattery" represents empty social graces; "Grandeur" and "Wealth" represent the emptiness of riches; "Office" represents the politics of society and fighting to get ahead; and the crowds seem to be unfeeling and unthinking.

3. Answers may vary slightly, but pay close attention to the distinction between the "proud" versus the "sacred." On one side, list those things related to pride. On the other, list those the speaker considers sacred.

4. Answers will vary. Although the speaker's intent is not to make a persuasive argument, his strong feelings could sway the listener to his way of thinking.

5. Answers will vary. This question should be thought of in terms of man's purpose. Is it to realize the self or to serve others?

CHAPTER 5: "The Charge of the Light Brigade" Alfred, Lord Tennyson (1809–1892)

1. The repetition of "half a league," with its emphasis on the first syllable, points toward exhaustion. "Theirs not to" in the second stanza notes confusion or deep thought, indicating a pause in the action. The repetition of "Cannon" in the third stanza comes across like a bombardment of artillery. And so on.

2. The words that rhyme within a stanza seem to relate to one another, emphasizing a particular thought. All the words that rhyme with "hundred" relate to the intensity of the battle or to wondering about it.

3. Some answers might be: Because Tennyson was Poet Laureate, it might have been improper for him to appear to criticize the military leaders. He might have wanted to keep the emphasis on the soldiers instead of the commander who messed up. Immediately after the battle, there was uncertainty as to who was to blame as the person who relayed the order died in the battle.

4. Answers will vary.

5. Answers will vary. You could take this same poem and show the Russians' viewpoint. By changing only a few words, you can show what the Russians thought of the charge they were seeing.

CHAPTER 6: "Vigil Strange I Kept on the Field One Night" Walt Whitman (1819–1892)

1. For example, lines 3 and 4 begin with the word "One." The entire poem appears to be one long sentence, but every line ends with some kind of punctuation to help the reader pause and reflect. Whitman shortens /ed/ words with an apostrophe even though it does not shorten the pronunciation. There are many more examples of form, so answers will vary.

2. *Night* signifies intimacy, as evidenced by the rich sensory descriptions of the night and the night-wind.

3. Most of the poem focuses on the fallen soldier. The thoughts in parentheses seem to be an internal conversation of the speaker.

4. Answers will vary. For an example of sensory imagery, refer to the answer to number 2 above.

5. Answers will vary. Consider the restrictions poets put on themselves when writing poetry in free verse.

CHAPTER 7: **"Because I Could Not Stop for Death"**
Emily Dickinson (1830–1886)

1. Stanza 1: Inciting incident that launches the story, introduces the main characters. Stanza 2: Develops the characters. Stanza 3: The action sequence, builds suspense about where they are going. You later realize that it is a flashback. Stanza 4: More suspense as the party arrives at a destination. Stanza 5: The climax of the story as the reader comes to grips with the concepts of time, memories, and eternity.

2. Look for words that relate to starting and stopping in each stanza.

3. The first is when Death picks her up, alluding to her actual passing from life into death. The second is at the graveside, signifying her passage into an eternal state. The woman never seems to realize she is passing through these stages.

4. Answers will vary.

5. Answers will vary.

CHAPTER 8: **"To an Athlete Dying Young"**
A. E. Housman (1859–1936)

1. Some examples to get you started are "your threshold" in line 7, "slip away" in line 9, and "shady night" in line 13. See if you can find at least five more euphemisms.

2. Don't forget to include repeated words such as "the" in the first line.

3. Answers will vary.

4. Answers will vary.

5. Answers will vary. Think about whether these individuals are remembered for a life of glorious living or a moment of glory before death.

Chapter Notes

CHAPTER 1: "Death, Be Not Proud"
John Donne (1572-1631)

1. "John Donne Sermons," *BYU Harold B. Lee Library Digital Collections*, 2013, <http://lib.byu.edu/digital/donne/> (February 25, 2013).

2. Bibhudutt Dash, "The Portrayal of Death in Donne's 'Death Be Not Proud' and Jaroslav Seifert's 'The Mistress of the Poets': A Comparative Study," *Language In India*, January 2012: 164+. *Literature Resource Center.* November 12, 2012, <http://go.galegroup.com/ps/i.do?id=GALE%7CA277602505&v=2.1&u=pwpls_remote&it=r&p=LitRC&sw=w> (February 25, 2013).

CHAPTER 2: "We Are Seven"
William Wordsworth (1770-1850)

1. William Knight, ed., *The Poetical Works of William Wordsworth, Volume I* (London: McMillan and Co. Ltd., 1896), accessed through Project Gutenberg, n.d., <http://www.gutenberg.org/ebooks/10219> (February 25, 2013).

2. Ibid.

3. Ibid.

4. Arthur H. Bell and Bernard D. N. Grebanier, *English Literature: 1800 to 1900. 2nd ed.* (Hauppauge, N.Y.: Barron's, 1994), p. 39.

CHAPTER 3: "No Coward Soul Is Mine"
Emily Brontë (1818-1848)

1. "Emily Bronte," Merriman, C. D. (2007: Jalic, Inc.), n.d., <http://www.online-literature.com/bronte/> (January 20, 2013).
2. Ephesians 6:10–17.
3. Ephesians 1:13, 14.
4. John 10:27-29.
5. Paola Enguix Fernández, "No Coward Soul Is Mine: Analysis of the Death andFaith in Emily Bronte's Poetry and Life," n.d., <http://mural.uv.es/paenfer/poesia/Emily%20Bronte.html> (December 15, 2012).

CHAPTER 4: "Good-by"
Ralph Waldo Emerson (1803-1882)

1. Ralph Waldo Emerson, "The Poet" from Essays, 2nd Series [1844], Texas A&M University, n.d., <http://transcendentalism.tamu.edu/authors/emerson/essays/poettext.html> (February 25, 2013).
2. Ralph Waldo Emerson, "The Transcendentalist: A Lecture Read at the Masonic Temple, Boston, January, 1842," (American Transcendental Web), Texas A&M University, n.d., <http://transcendentalism.tamu.edu/authors/emerson/essays/transcendentalist.html> (January 16, 2013).
3. Ibid.
4. Cliff Tilloston, "The Correspondence Between Ralph Waldo Emerson and Thomas Carlyle," *Institute of World Culture*, July 2011, <http://www.worldculture.org/articles/EmersonCarlyle_Tillotson.pdf> (February 20, 2013).

CHAPTER 5: "The Charge of the Light Brigade" Alfred, Lord Tennyson (1809-1892)

1. William Howard Russell, "The Charge of the Light Brigade," The Times/1854/News/The Charge of the Light Brigade, n.d., <http://en.wikisource.org/wiki/The_Charge_of_the_Light_Brigade_%28article%29> (February 17, 2013).

2. General Lord George Paget, "The Battle of Balaclava," Extracts from the Letters and Journal of General Lord George Paget, 1881, *Victorian Web.org*, n.d., <http://www.victorianweb.org/history/crimea/paget/pagetbala.html> (February 17, 2013).

CHAPTER 6: "Vigil Strange I Kept on the Field One Night" Walt Whitman (1819-1892)

1. Gutman Huck, "Drum-Taps" (1865), *The Walt Whitman Archive*, Select Criticism, n.d., <http://whitmanarchive.org/criticism/current/encyclopedia/entry_83.html> (February 25, 2013).

2. Martin G. Murray, "Traveling With the Wounded: Walt Whitman and Washington's Civil War Hospitals," originally published in *Washington History: Magazine of the Historical Society of Washington, D.C.* 8 (Fall/Winter 1996–1997), 58–73, 92–93, accessed through *The Walt Whitman Archive*, n.d., <http://whitmanarchive.org/criticism/current/anc.00156.html> (February 25, 2013).

3. Angel Price, "Whitman's Drum Taps and Washington's Civil War Hospitals," University of Virginia, n.d., <http://xroads.virginia.edu/~cap/hospital/whitman.htm> (February 17, 2013).

CHAPTER 7: "Because I Could Not Stop for Death" Emily Dickinson (1830-1886)

1. "Emily Dickinson (1830–1886)," *Nineteenth-Century Literature Criticism*. Ed. Jessica Bomarito and Russel Whitaker. Vol. 171. Detroit: Thomson Gale, 2007, 84–233. Literature Criticism Online, Gale 12 November 2012 [Page 171], n.d., <http://galenet.galegroup.com/servlet/LitCrit/pwpls_remote/FJ2680850003> (February 13, 2013).

2. Thomas Wentworth Higginson, "Emily Dickinson's Letters," *Atlantic Magazine,* October 1891, 2013, <http://www.theatlantic.com/magazine/archive/1891/10/emily-dickinsons-letters/306524/#> (February 25, 2013).

CHAPTER 8: "To an Athlete Dying Young" A. E. Housman (1859-1936)

1. Arthur H. Bell and Bernard D. N. Grebanier, *English Literature: 1800 to 1900. 2nd ed.* (Hauppauge, N.Y.: Barron's, 1994), p. 293.

2. "A. E. Housman," *Poets.org,* 1997–2012, <http://www.poets.org/poet.php/prmPID/631> (February 17, 2013).

Glossary

Age of Enlightenment—An intellectual movement begun in England in the late seventeenth century that focused on the power and goodness of human reason. Writers prized developing knowledge over feelings and character.

alliteration—A poetic device that has words close together in a poem begin with the same sound or letters.

allusion—Reference to something outside a poem. The reference is meant to provide extra information without having to describe it in the poem.

anaphora—The repetition of a word or phrase at the beginning of successive clauses.

apostrophe—When someone or something is addressed that is not physically there.

Church of England—The established church in England, founded when Henry VIII broke away from the Roman Catholic Church by declaring he was the rightful head of the church in England, not the pope.

conceit—An elaborate comparison, often taking the form of an extended metaphor.

couplet—Each set of two lines in a poem.

curate—The name for a priest in the Church of England. A curate could be further designated a rector, a vicar, or a perpetual curate. The distinction depended on who appointed him the position within the church and where the money to pay him came from.

dactyl—A metrical foot consisting of one stressed syllable followed by two unstressed syllables.

dimeter—A line of verse consisting of two metrical feet.

elision—The omission of a syllable to make a line of poetry fit a specific meter. An apostrophe is used to replace the omitted syllable.

euphemism—A mild word used to reference something unpleasant.

extended metaphor—A metaphor that extends through all or several lines of a work.

foot—A metrical unit consisting of a stressed syllable with its companion unstressed syllables.

foreshadow—To suggest an event before it happens.

iamb—A unit of one unaccented syllable followed by an accented syllable.

iambic pentameter—A meter with five feet in a line. Each foot has an unstressed syllable followed by a stressed syllable.

irony—When the meaning implied is different from the literal meaning of the words used. Irony relies on context to help the reader understand the implied meaning.

metaphor—A symbolic comparison or representation used in literature to convey additional meaning by relating an object or concept to something that is already known.

meter—The number of beats, or stressed syllables, in a line of poetry.

octave—A group of eight lines of poetry.

paradox—The use of ideas that contradict one another but work together toward a deeper insight when placed side by side.

pentameter—A meter with five feet per line.

personification—Giving human attributes to something that is nonhuman.

Protestant—Any group of Christians who separated from the Roman Catholic Church, or bodies of Christians derived from them.

Puritan—A group of people in sixteenth- and seventeenth-century England who wanted to purify the church of ungodly practices. They believed in working to change the church from within rather than breaking away completely.

quatrain—A group of four lines of poetry.

refrain—Lines repeated in a poem or song, usually at the end of each verse.

rhyme scheme—The pattern of rhyme in poetry, usually described with sets of letters such as *abba* or *abab*; lines with the same letter rhyme.

sestet—Two sets of tercets; six lines of poetry.

simile—A comparison of two dissimilar things using *like* or *as*.

sonnet—A poem of fourteen lines that uses a formal rhyme scheme. Sonnets written in English often have ten syllables per line, known as iambic pentameter.

stanza—A group of lines forming the basic recurring metrical unit in a poem. Also called a verse.

synecdoche—A literary device where a part of something stands for the whole of it.

tercet—A group of three lines of poetry.

visual rhyme—Occurs when words are spelled similarly but do not rhyme audibly. Also called eye rhyme or sight rhyme.

Further Reading

Books

Andronik, Catherine M. *Wildly Romantic: The English Romantic Poets—The Mad, the Bad, the Dangerous.* New York: Henry Holt and Co., 2007.

Bloom, Harold. *Till I End My Song: A Gathering of Last Poems.* New York: HarperCollins, 2010.

Ladd, Andrew, and Jerry Phillips, ed. *Romanticism and Transcendentalism: 1800–1860.* New York: Facts on File, 2006.

Parisi, Joseph, and Stephen Young, eds. *The Poetry Anthology.* Chicago: Ivan R. Dee, 2004.

Internet Addresses

The Poetry Foundation: Poems & Poets
<http://www.poetryfoundation.org/browse/>

Poets.org: Poems for Teens
<http://www.poets.org/viewmedia.php/prmMID/20785>

Index